A Call for Engaged Leadership

TRANSGRESSIONS: CULTURAL STUDIES AND EDUCATION
Volume 91

TRANSGRESSIONS: CULTURAL STUDIES AND EDUCATION

Cultural studies provides an analytical toolbox for both making sense of educational practice and extending the insights of educational professionals into their labors. In this context *Transgressions: Cultural Studies and Education* provides a collection of books in the domain that specify this assertion. Crafted for an audience of teachers, teacher educators, scholars and students of cultural studies and others interested in cultural studies and pedagogy, the series documents both the possibilities of and the controversies surrounding the intersection of cultural studies and education. The editors and the authors of this series do not assume that the interaction of cultural studies and education devalues other types of knowledge and analytical forms. Rather the intersection of these knowledge disciplines offers a rejuvenating, optimistic, and positive perspective on education and educational institutions. Some might describe its contribution as democratic, emancipatory, and transformative. The editors and authors maintain that cultural studies helps free educators from sterile, monolithic analyses that have for too long undermined efforts to think of educational practices by providing other words, new languages, and fresh metaphors. Operating in an interdisciplinary cosmos, Transgressions: Cultural Studies and Education is dedicated to exploring the ways cultural studies enhances the study and practice of education. With this in mind the series focuses in a non-exclusive way on popular culture as well as other dimensions of cultural studies including social theory, social justice and positionality, cultural dimensions of technological innovation, new media and media literacy, new forms of oppression emerging in an electronic hyperreality, and postcolonial global concerns. With these concerns in mind cultural studies scholars often argue that the realm of popular culture is the most powerful educational force in contemporary culture. Indeed, in the twenty-first century this pedagogical dynamic is sweeping through the entire world. Educators, they believe, must understand these emerging realities in order to gain an important voice in the pedagogical conversation.

Without an understanding of cultural pedagogy's (education that takes place outside of formal schooling) role in the shaping of individual identity – youth identity in particular – the role educators play in the lives of their students will continue to fade. Why do so many of our students feel that life is incomprehensible and devoid of meaning? What does it mean, teachers wonder, when young people are unable to describe their moods, their affective affiliation to the society around them. Meanings provided young people by mainstream institutions often do little to help them deal with their affective complexity, their difficulty negotiating the rift between meaning and affect. School knowledge and educational expectations seem as anachronistic as a ditto machine, not that learning ways of rational thought and making sense of the world are unimportant.

But school knowledge and educational expectations often have little to offer students about making sense of the way they feel, the way their affective lives are shaped. In no way do we argue that analysis of the production of youth in an electronic mediated world demands some "touchy-feely" educational superficiality. What is needed in this context is a rigorous analysis of the interrelationship between pedagogy, popular culture, meaning making, and youth subjectivity. In an era marked by youth depression, violence, and suicide such insights become extremely important, even life saving. Pessimism about the future is the common sense of many contemporary youth with its concomitant feeling that no one can make a difference.

If affective production can be shaped to reflect these perspectives, then it can be reshaped to lay the groundwork for optimism, passionate commitment, and transformative educational and political activity. In these ways cultural studies adds a dimension to the work of education unfilled by any other sub-discipline. This is what Transgressions: Cultural Studies and Education seeks to produce—literature on these issues that makes a difference. It seeks to publish studies that help those who work with young people, those individuals involved in the disciplines that study children and youth, and young people themselves improve their lives in these bizarre times.

A Call for Engaged Leadership

Cornell Thomas
Texas Christian University, USA

SENSE PUBLISHERS
ROTTERDAM/BOSTON/TAIPEI

A C.I.P. record for this book is available from the Library of Congress.

ISBN: 978-94-6209-111-5 (paperback)
ISBN: 978-94-6209-112-2 (hardback)
ISBN: 978-94-6209-113-9 (e-book)

Published by: Sense Publishers,
P.O. Box 21858,
3001 AW Rotterdam,
The Netherlands
https://www.sensepublishers.com/

Printed on acid-free paper

TABLE OF CONTENTS

INTRODUCTION

Do nothing out of selfish ambition or vain conceit, but in humility consider others better than yourselves. Each of you should look not only to your own interests, but also to the interests of others. Your attitude should be the same as that of Christ Jesus: Who, being in very nature God, did not consider equality with God something to be grasped, but made himself nothing, taking the very nature of a servant, being made in human likeness (Philippians 2: 3–7).

Our church once used the slogan, "Saved to Serve." This slogan speaks to my personal understanding of my walk with God and how it shapes who I am in all aspects of life, including as a leader.

I profess to be a child of God. I pray each day to be in His will and that through the actions of this body He will be glorified. I work to give all of me back to Him.

The birth, life, death and resurrection of Jesus shares God's love for each of us and also brings great clarity to how we should love each other. Through His great love, God sent his son as an atoning sacrifice for our sins. I strive to be the best in all that I do as a husband, father, grandfather, son, sibling, friend, professor, administrator, by dedicating my life to the Father each day. I pray that His will, not mine, be done and that He uses me to share just how good the fruit of the spirit can be in ones' life.

More specifically, I look at the good in an individual, at the gifts provided to them and begin relationships from this premise. Each relationship is built on a desire to serve others in ways that lead to the sharing of my faith. During this process the depth of my own understanding of God deepens.

My walk with God also informs and controls the way I lead. The role of leadership is indeed one of service. It is working to clear pathways to facilitate the work of others. Christ has provided a pathway leading back to the Father. The Holy Spirit provides guidance along this pathway, for those who seek God's way. The foundation of my desire for leadership is anchored by service to others and on the goal to provide influence, direction and be a part of a community of believers that leads us to a more fulfilling life. While we can bring personal understanding to what we mean by a more fulfilling life, we know that this life is indeed empty when God is not in the center.

God was in the center of my father's life. My father's life has provided me with an earthly model to follow. I will share some brief thoughts of my father in closing.

I wrote something to honor my father when he went home to be with God. This is, in part, what I said. "I don't know how my father lived his early days. I do not know much about the type of person he was, though I have heard some stories.

But, I do know the person he became. Galatians 5:22 best describes for me the spirit that shone through this body of Eugene Thomas."

> But when the Holy Spirit controls our lives he will produce this kind of fruit in us: love, joy, peace, patience, kindness, goodness, faithfulness, gentleness and self-control...

My father was a planter and harvester of the seeds of the spirit. He was full of love. My father shared his joy and faith in God with everyone that came around him. He did this not just in words but also in his actions. God used my father in ways that brought glory to Him. My father's walk with God also brought his family closer to the Lord. Indeed, he helped each of us become planters and harvesters of the seed of the spirit. I hope and pray that the same can be said of me at my home going.

Other individual live by a variety of faiths, based on a religion, science, greed, the desire to win, or just themselves. It is the premise of this book that leadership should be focused on serving others in inclusive ways. Leadership should, as a primary task, help to create pathways that allow others to complete the work at hand and to do so including all voices in the process.

This is the premise that guides the words presented in this book.

Cornell Thomas

A CALL FOR ENGAGED LEADERSHIP

Another school year will begin soon. Children will be walking through classroom doors full of excitement and anticipation. The doors of knowledge will open wide and students will be ready to eagerly embrace all that their teachers are prepared to share. Teachers too will be excited about the start of the school year and will be looking forward to implementing the great teaching and learning strategies they have planned for their students. There is a wealth of positive energy and high expectations for student success from teachers, parents and the students themselves.

This scenario paints a picture of schooling that we all want to believe is true at every school. However this is not the case in most urban schools.

> The persistent failure of urban schools and repeated efforts to change them have shaped much of the debate about education policy in the United States over the past forty years. The issues have remained stubbornly constant: inadequate funding and resources, unequal educational opportunity, high dropout rates and low academic achievement, student alienation, racial segregation, and race and class inequality within and among urban schools (Lipman, 2004, p. 5).

Many children entering school this year continue to come from homes where parents are ill prepared to provide the kinds of intellectually stimulating experiences that improve their children's chances of success in the classroom. In many of these homes the knowledge needed to nurture and support the academic growth of children is limited. Many of these parents do not read to, and with their children; they do not frequent the library, zoo, science or history museums, or other venues that promote learning. These parents have not had these kinds of experiences themselves to share with their children. They work hard to make ends meet and only visit the school if there is a problem with their sons or daughters. These parents, while doing the best they can, are not equipped to help their children excel academically.

Here is another scenario. Truman Elementary is a K-5 school set amidst a lower and middle-income housing tract that was constructed on the southwest side of the city in 1948. Once a typical middle-class neighborhood, Truman is now populated by few of the original, now aging residents, and a growing transient population of low-income renters. The school has a high proportion of Aid to Family with Dependent Children recipients among its 502 ethnically diverse students. About 80 percent of the school's children are Hispanic, 10 percent are Anglo, and the remainder are African-American and relatively recent Asian immigrants.

Over eighty percent of the faculty has taught at Truman for ten years or more. Ninety percent of the faculty has had at least five years of teaching experience at Truman, while the remaining ten percent have less than five years of experience, all at Truman. Of the twenty teachers at Truman, sixteen classify themselves as Anglo, three Hispanic (all teaching in bilingual classrooms), and there is one who classifies herself as African-American. All of the staff, custodians, aides, cafeteria workers, are either Hispanic or African-American.

You have been transferred to Truman as the new principal. Soon after your arrival you encounter a fragmented staff who consistently communicates (1) that they feel no support from leadership, and (2) most of the children are 'at risk' due to factors outside the control of the school. There are extensive disciplinary problems, uneven, but overall low student achievement, and a laundry list of other irritants, ranging from the types of students in gifted and talented classes versus special education classes, to teacher gripes about not having enough supplies, math manipulatives and computer software. The former principal, and a few of the old vanguard, tried to hold on to the traditions that had made Truman an outstanding academic institution in years past. Now, instead of working as a team, teachers were guarding their turf and ignoring other challenges impacting the school.

One of the biggest challenges that has now led the State to identify Truman as a school to take over, is that of Truman students having the lowest performance on state mandated tests for the past several years. To make matters worse, many of the teachers at Truman view the parents of their students as an anchor around their children's ankles, sinking them to depths that make academic excellence virtually impossible.

This attitude about these parents and their children has been prevalent in urban schools for decades. These same negative opinions about the parents of the children they teach are growing rapidly in our suburban public schools. What a shame. We have created an environment, perceptual and real, where teachers, administrators and students are oppressed in so many ways. Many of these individuals have a diminishing sense of hope. They lack strong convictions that support high levels of student success, and the same belief in themselves. Excuses become the primary mode of discussion. Teachers blame parents, principals blame teachers, students just hate school, and parents are clueless. What a terrible rationale for simply teaching to a state mandated test for the entire academic year! Even more, what a poor excuse for lowering the expectations of students!

Presented here is a school with the kinds of challenges faced in many public schools, both suburban and urban.

- What are the major challenges that must be addressed by the principal at Truman?;
- How will these challenges be identified?; and
- What should be the role of the various stakeholders?

It seems appropriate to provide a brief overview of leadership theories before addressing these and other questions.

LEADERSHIP THEORY

Hundreds of books on leadership have been written. A major theme in most, if not all, of these books is focused on how a successful leader organizes people to get the task at hand accomplished. These discussions resulted in research focused on identifying the characteristics that leaders possessed. Much of this work studied those considered to be the great leaders, past and present. The "trait theory of leadership" is considered one of the first leadership theories to be identified in the literature. This theory provided the foundation upon which leadership was researched, defined and explained. Most noted was Thomas Carlyle's (1841) Heroes and Hero Worship, and Francis Galton's (1869) Hereditary Genius. Carlyle's work attempted to identify the primary talents, skills and even physical attributes needed for successful leadership. Galton's work studied the families of those considered to be great leaders. He believed that leadership was inherited.

Studies focused on leadership in the late 1940's and early 1950's began to challenge the trait leadership theory. Results from these research efforts began to say that individuals emerge as leaders across a smorgasbord of situations. Since then, a multitude of leadership theories have been delineated. The Behavioral theories of Skinner, McClelland, and Lewin, Lipitt and White were embraced by many in the field of leadership. Other theories have come, gone, and come again. Among these are the contingency theory, a behavioral model based on the premise that there is no one best way to lead. Effective and successful leadership must consider the external and internal factors influencing the organization. Transactional (based on the premise that the individual is motivated by reward and punishment), servant (based on the premise that both the organization and the employees are important; there is a strong emphasis on community building and empowerment; argues that service is the primary function of the leadership), and transformational (based on the premise that effective leadership is built on the ability to intellectually stimulate and inspirationally motivate individuals to higher levels of attainment) theories. Embedded in these works are discussions regarding every element of an organization, from the organizational structure, culture, arguments attempting to distinguish between managers and leaders, and the group dynamics. All of these discussions stress the complexity regarding leadership and how a person becomes, or is born to be, an effective leader. Yet much of the research has attempted to define leadership in less complex ways.

Many of us grew up from childhood learning to understand, for example, right from wrong, good or bad, smart or dumb, strong or weak, pretty or ugly, acceptance or rejection. Sharing was a right thing to do, while selfishness was bad. Following directions from your parents and teachers was a good thing to do, but hitting your sibling was bad. You were rewarded for the smart things that you did, and punished for your actions that were considered dumb. The strongest person won the trophy, the weakest got dirt kicked in their face. Those considered pretty (handsome) got all of the attention, while those considered ugly would be marginalized most all the time. If you were considered good in these ways, then you were accepted by those in control. All others were deemed different and not included in the inner circles of the main group. They were also not considered leadership material.

These straightforward examples of treatment based on either/or descriptors are at the root of many of the ills of our society today, and in our public schools. Seemingly basic, clear-cut ways of making sense of the world plague our attempts to value anyone that seems to be different. This approach has caused many of us in this society to think of gays, racial groups, non-Christians, and those with a disability for example, as less than. Thinking in this way has led to a sense of alienation for so many citizens in this country. This thinking is also the root cause of many of the challenges faced in today's classrooms. Max Stirner talks about "Wheels In The Head." He refers to a thought that a person cannot give up as a "Wheel In The Head", which in turn controls an individual's will and uses the individual rather than being used by the individual. Are these Wheels similar to the social constructs in this society that allow negative stereotypic images of people control what we think of them and tell some of us our potential for success based merely on our perceived race or social economic status? Are these Wheels similar to the social constructs in this society that provide the rationales some educators employ to justify remedial programs, tracking, rote teaching processes, and high stakes testing? Are these Wheels similar to the social constructs in this society that have created gatekeepers (IQ tests, statewide high stakes testing, and college entrance level exams) that limit entrance for so many individuals in our society into the ivory towers of higher education? I would suggest that they do. Stirner suggests a need to transgress from the educated person where knowledge is the determiner of choice to the free person where knowledge is the source of greater choice (Spring, 1994, pg. 44). What is most alarming is that differences are attributed to individuals based merely on socially constructed group identifiers. Identifiers based on false data. How can school leaders right these wrongs? This paper supports the premise that one way to right these wrongs in our schools is for leaders to embrace the concept of principal as an engaged leader.

Thomas Friedman (The World Is Flat), Jim Collins (Good To Great) and Malcolm Gladwell (Blink) represent authors recently espousing the need for future leaders with the abilities to work successfully with people from all walks of life. While taking more of a business approach, they are speaking to "The Beloved Community" attributed to Dr. Martin Luther King, Jr. and supported by so many others, including this author. This premise points to the importance of broadening our perspectives regarding differences and how these different ways of seeing, doing and living can bring new synergy and greater success to organizations, and in this case, schools. We need leaders who are willing to transgress current belief and behaviors.

New Webster's Dictionary defines transgress: to go beyond; to act in violation of; to step across. Most of us would consider transgressions to be against the law; to be a negative action. Yet it seems that most, if not all, great discoveries emerged because someone chose to go beyond; take a different path; and stepping across the standard ways of doing and thinking. For us to transgress means to begin anew, to imagine the possibilities of how things can improve, and to move forward in new and creative ways. We suggest that, when looking at school leadership, now is the time to transgress.

As stated before, there are numerous theories that attempt to define leadership and clarify the role of the leader. It is suggested here that most, if not all, of these theories enhance a person's ability to lead. However, leaders should strive to take from all of these theories and to not fully embrace just one. Leaders need to broaden their perspectives about leadership on a continual basis. Leaders need to take their knowledge of leadership and employ the skills needed to accomplish goals, given the situation. Embedded in this work is the need for more emphasis being placed on the importance of relationships from an individual versus group perspective, as a way to help empower individuals to excel in their work. Hollander reminds us, "Reaching leadership at the next level means "doing things with people, rather than to people," which is the essence of inclusion....It also provides an atmosphere that promotes fairness of input and output to all (Hollander, 2008, p. 3).

The call here is to believe that in today's work environment successful leaders must recognize the individual more now than the group, or groups within an organization. Understanding the importance of each individual in an organization and using the attributes that they bring to the team is indeed a challenging and, for some, a daunting task. It is posited here that this task can be successfully accomplished when leaders embrace the concept of principal as engaged leader. Leaders in today's school environments must continue to listen, learn and better utilize the knowledge and skills of other stakeholders. These leaders must be able to function in an ever evolving teaching and learning environment. Similar to the ethos of engaged pedagogy, engaged leadership assumes that every stakeholder has valuable contributions to make that will improve the organization. The engaged leader inspires participation, encourages meaningful working relationships between stakeholders, and is enthusiastic about the possibilities that emerge from this type of dynamic, interactive, inclusive process. The proposition here is that leadership must be inclusive of the voices of all stakeholders. When stakeholders are fully engaged, the organization becomes a more interactive, exciting, transformative, progressive, productive, and successful teaching and learning environment. In this type of environment everyone has opportunities to contribute in positive ways. Most, if not all, individuals grow in this kind of environment. They become more empowered advocates for the success of the organization, and develop their own leadership skills. The engaged leader helps to create the kind of teaching and learning environment that causes others to critically examine their own perspectives, question those perspectives with others within the organization, and move towards more improved teaching and learning.

The premise presented here states that in order to increase the productivity of an organization, leaders must move away from generalized understandings of people and their jobs, to more of an individual, personal approach. Within larger organizations, this work is done with direct reports who in turn embrace this same approach with their direct reports. Of course leaders find opportunities to interact with other members of the team in similar ways. Max DePree, in Leadership is an Art, puts it this way when looking at leadership with an elegant (great) company:

> Most of the time, when we consider ourselves and others, we are looking at only one part of people. The measure of individuals-and so of corporations-is the extent to which we struggle to complete ourselves, the energy we devote to living up to our potential. An elegant company frees its members to be their best. Elegant leaders free the people they meet to do the same (DePree, 1990, pg. 142.).

In other words, this premise calls for leadership that looks for the good in an individual, at the gifts provided to them, and begin relationships from this premise. Each relationship is built on a desire to serve others in ways that lead to actions that support the mission of the organization in very positive, productive ways. Engaged leaders are part teacher using a Socratic approach, mediator of group discussions, and activator of the goals that emerge from this work.

> Spock:....Were I to invoke logic, however, logic clearly dictates that the needs of the many outweigh the needs of the few.

> Kirk:... Or the one.

> Star Trek: The Wrath of Khan

The role of leadership is indeed one of growing complexity. Yet, it is still focused on working to clear pathways to facilitate the work of others. Leadership understands that the needs of the many are most important. That process varies given the unique dynamics at play. Yes, all aspects of leadership should be considered and utilized as needed. Undergirding decisions should be a desire for leadership that is anchored by service to others and on the goal to provide influence, direction, and be a part of a community of individuals dedicated to the mission of the organization. Yet there are times when decisions must be made. External and internal factors often call for a multifaceted approach to leadership. The discussions that follow will attempt to bring clarity to our variety of approaches to leadership and change.

REFERENCES

Burns, J.M. (1978). Leadership. New York: Harper & Row.

Cawelti, G. (1994). Behavior Patterns of Effective Principals. Educational Leadership, 42. 3.

Collins, J. (2001). Good to Great: Why Some Companies Make the Leap... and Others Don't. New York: HarperCollins.

DePree, M. (1990). Leadership is an Art. New York: Crown Publishing.

Edmonds, R. (1979). Effective schools for the urban poor. Educational Leadership, 37, 15–24.

Friedman, T. (2005). The World Is Flat: A Brief History of the Twenty-first Centure. New York: Farrer, Straus, and Giroux.

Gladwell, M. (2005). Blink: The Power of Thinking Without Thinking. New York: Little, Brown and Company.

Hollander, E. (2008). Inclusive Leadership: The Essential Leader – Follower Relationship. New York: Taylor and Francis.

Hoy, W. and Miskel, C. (1996). Educational Administration: Theory Research and Practice. New York: McGraw-Hill, Inc.

Leithwood, K. (February 1992). "The Move Toward Transformational Leadership." Educational Leadership, pp. 8–12.

Lipham, J. (1981). Effective principal, effective school. National Association of Secondary School Principals Bulletin.

Lipham, P. (2004). High Stakes Education: Inequality, Globalization, and Urban School Reform. New York: RoutledgeFalmer.

Shulman, L. (2002). Making Differences: A Table of Learning. Change, 34, 36–45.

Spring, J. (1994). Wheels In The Head. New York: McGraw-Hill.

CHAPTER 3

A CALL FOR ENGAGED LEADERSHIP

A Personal Perspective

I would often wonder what it would be like to become a college president. As I secured tenure, promotion to associate professor and department chair, my curiosity grew. So, I began to read all that I could regarding the college presidency and attend presidential leadership institutes and other sessions on the topic. I also began asking presidents who I met to share some of their experiences with me. One of the sessions focused on the college presidency provided mentors for all participants for one year. This president shared numerous experiences with me. I want to share some of his experiences with you.

Martin, not his real name, told me that he turned down a college presidency within the same denomination to serve another considered to be the most problematic. Dr. Palmer said that he accepted the fact at the college had a history of fiscal deficits, poor retention statistics, infrastructure issues, and very low graduation rates. The college was small with an enrollment averaging about 600 undergraduate students. The majority of the student population, about eighty-five percent, were considered at-risk in high school. They were not academically qualified for successful admission into most four year institutions. The same could be said regarding faculty. Most of the faculty could not secure similar positions at other four year institutions. Most of them did not work to remain informed of new developments in their area of study and did little in the area of research. So they settled for lower salaries, under-motivated students, and limited resources. There were a few outstanding faculty who had decided to devote their life's work in this type of college. Their work was excellent and could be compared favorably with other individuals in some of the very best institutions of higher education across the country. Martin believed that this college presidency was more than a mere job. He thought of this position as his ministry. Martin had experienced a full career in some very well respected institutions of higher education and truly believed that it was now time to give back to those who represented members of poor and disadvantaged communities similar to his own origins. He also thought that he could lead a process that would turn this college inside-out. Dr. Palmer thought that by developing a superior honors program, hiring a few new faculty to teach in this new program, and offering excellent scholarships to attract academically strong students a foundation for institutional change would begin. Martin dedicated all of his energy to develop a leadership team made up of students, staff, faculty and community stakeholders that would move this college forward to become a good liberal arts institution in a somewhat short period of time and an excellent one in the near future. Dr. Palmer thought that financial support from foundations, corporations and philanthropic leaders in the community would follow once the college had a powerful story of success to share. He then told me about other challenges that were discovered soon after accepting the position.

Martin decided to set aside one hour time allotments to meet with each of his direct reports, and a few key faculty and administrators over the first few days of his administration. As you might expect, every meeting lasted well over the hour that was allotted. Much to his surprise, Dr. Palmer found that most of them lacked the knowledge and skill set to hold the position that they were in. For example the person responsible for student affairs had only two years of experience in education. She had no knowledge of student development theories, no understanding of programming for students, and ran her department as if it were a correctional facility. Even the rules, which were selectively enforced, we're archaic. There were no visitation periods for students, a ten o'clock curfew, no peer mediation process, and monetary fines for those found breaking the rules. Student activities were poorly organized, with little input from students. Discussions lead to the conclusion that most activities were put together at the last minute. The former president did not even allocate funds from student activity fees to support any initiatives in this department. Martin was told that historically they had to be tough with the students in order to get them to obey the rules. Most of the staff in this department also lacked the knowledge, skills and experience to do a good job. They seemed more prepared to serve as prison guards. The kind of prison guards who typically look the other way when bad things occurred. Those few that had some valuable contributions to make were threatened and either left the college or remained quiet to keep their job. Many of them seemed to lacked the common sense to know that what they were doing was actually reinforcing the very behaviors and negative habits that they wanted students to change. Rumors were rampant regarding the activities of some of the hall directors. Primarily, rumors focused on hall directors having sex with students. While it took some time to confirm, once the truth was known people were released. Martin was shocked by what he was learning and seeing. When walking the campus for the first time as president, he told those with him that he felt like he was walking through the third ward in Houston, Texas. Student's pants, male and female, we're sagging below the butt, young ladies wore as little as possible, it seemed that just about every student talked loudly with cursing being the norm. Many of the students looked drugged. Many staff members, except those the students called 5-0, seemed afraid of the students on campus and avoided potential confrontational situations. The cafeteria reminded Martin of a prison mess hall. All tables were in a straight row, students dragged in and out and slumped over their food as they ate – between loud talking, laughing, and cursing with other students across the room. What a sight. What a rude awakening to this campus called a college. Security and residence hall managers positioned themselves in preparation of the inevitable fights that often erupted. Martin began to wonder if he had made the right decision.

One academic administrator was proud of the math and vocabulary flash card program that she established. She encouraged all faculty to participate in this program during the first ten minutes of class. Please remember, this is a college! Another administrator spent his mornings checking to see if faculty arrived at work by eight o'clock each day, wether they taught that day or not. He demonstrated great excitement when talking about the disciplinary write-ups for those who were late. Mind you, nothing was done with these write-ups. His supervisor, the vice president for academic affairs, simply stated that this was an accommodation, a show of respect for this elderly gentleman. The vice president for academic affairs did not see a need for a great deal of professional development activities. Therefore no funds were allocated for faculty to travel to present their research or to simply participate at state, regional, national or international conferences. No professional development activities included outside presenters. Instead activities focused on the importance of taking class attendance, grade reporting, health insurance updates, and policy changes. It seems that the same agenda was simply recycled for the start of each academic year.

The chief financial officer had a degree in History. He had moved up the ranks in the business where he started as a cashier after graduating from the college many years ago. The development officer was a very good friend of the former president who boldly shared that his largest gift to the college, $25,000.00, was given by his fraternity two years ago. I am simply sharing the facts here, with no exaggerations.

Martin was equally surprised to discover that board leadership said that he knew nothing about the depth of these issues. As a matter of fact, Martin was accused of exaggerating these and other issues and was told by board leadership to relax, that he was not use to this type of college environment and, after some time, would get used to it.

Retention and graduation rates over the past six years were much worse than reported. Both were in single digits. After more discussions and review of real data, Martin realized that more than eighty-five percent of the students currently enrolled read at or below the fifth grade level. Similar findings were found regarding basic mathematics. Most students were repeating remedial level courses, or simply did not return. Student attendance in class was horrible. Actually students with good attendance were guaranteed passing by some faculty despite incomplete assignments and failed examinations. Academic leadership explained that they had to show some level of success in order to remain accredited. They blamed recruitment staff and the former president for the quality of students attending the college. A review of student credentials confirmed these beliefs, but did not make Martin support the actions of academic leadership. A preview of transcripts told him that over twenty percent of the students currently enrolled had taken a special education curriculum in high school, making their 3.0 and better grade point averages questionable. Yet many of these students started with academic scholarships, which were soon lost, at the college. Well over fifty percent of students graduated from alternative high schools. About ten percent entered college with GED certificates. The majority of the remainder graduated from their respective high schools in the lower twenty percent. These high schools represented those considered some of the lowest performing in the entire state. Deans lacked leadership skills, adequate knowledge of subject matter in their teaching areas and had no plans in place to make improvements of such a deplorable situation.

After more research Martin found that documents sent to the state and federal agencies were full of misleading data. The academic challenges were indeed far worse than reported and initially believed. Martin wondered how the doors of the college managed to remain open all of these years. It was the misleading reporting of data that seemed to keep officials from the kind of analysis that would have lead to probationary status. Actually it seemed as if no one really cared. There were a few faculty who really tried to teach. Records told Martin that most of them lasted one or two years. Those that remained were paid poorly but earned less than they were paid. Members of the faculty constantly complained about low pay, horrible students, the crumbling infrastructure, lack of adequate supplies and little to no up to date technology. Yet they remained year after year applying at other institutions, but failing to secure other positions. There were few that really demonstrated that they cared for the students and the college, but instruction and content was dumbed down, often below high school standards. The nightmare became more vivid as Martin continued to ferret through the lies and half-truths of his direct reports and others. Conversations with students made clear their lack of preparedness for college, or even a real high school curriculum. There was no way that they should be enrolled in college at this time. They needed a great deal of remedial work before attending college.

Dr. Palmer also discovered that the college was running budget deficits for each of the past six years. Funds from the endowment had been withdrawn each summer to cover these deficits. These withdrawals and recent economic downturns had depleted well over sixty percent of the endowment. One had to wonder if restricted dollars had been used inappropriately. Martin discovered the misuse of federal and state funding of well over one million dollars. The college had to borrow funds to cover what state auditors forced the college to repay and to corrective misuse of federal funding before a federal audit was conducted. He also found well over an estimated ten million dollars in deferred maintenance. He just could not understand why the college never established funding budgets for deferred maintenance. Every building on campus was in need of major repairs. The college administrators also failed to establish an annual capital budget. It became very clear to Martin, after asking chief financial officers from other organizations to conduct mini audits that the college was on the verge of financial collapse.

Trustees were asked to attend a retreat conducted by one of the financial consultants to better understand the college's financial challenges and approve a plan to address these concerns that Martin and his team had developed with the help of his three financial consultant friends. Many board members were shocked at the findings. Some apologized for their lack of due diligence over the years. The plan was approved by the trustees, but continuously challenged by board leadership, despite the gradual improvements that were shared. The plan established standard accounting practices in the business office that included balancing the books monthly instead of annually, yes I said annually – just before the annual audit! Monitoring spending variances became a monthly standard practice, along with calculating annual revenue streams. The student recruitment plan, including targeting specific programs for growth, would bring focus to recruiting better prepared students, resulting in better retention and enrollment projections. The college consolidated bank accounts to secure better rates, and implemented better budget building processes to estimate more precise revenue and expenditure projections. President Palmer also negotiated several contracts with companies that the college outsources services, implemented an energy savings program, and selected vendors offering more competitive rates. This small campus began to see significant savings immediately. The college actually ended Dr. Palmer's third year as president with a $1.2 million dollar surplus.

Martin, after developing some positive relationships, learned that people in the surrounding community called the college Hood U. They were pleased with the changes that were taking place and believed that the institution just might become a real college in the near future. A few felt that the campus was now safe enough to attend sporting and musical events.

The strategic plan developed in partnership with stakeholders (trustees, students, staff, faculty, alumni officers, and community leaders) called for three major initiatives.

- Establish a more engaging and rigorous academic environment
- Develop a process leading to financial sustainability
- Improve the physical plant

After two years the following goals from the strategic plan were accomplished:

ESTABLISH A MORE ENGAGING AND RIGOROUS ACADEMIC ENVIRONMENT

Established the Office of Student Academic Success. Services provided through this office include:

- Opened the Office of Student Academic Assistance
- Provide free tutors for every subject and course
- Provide workshops to improve study, note taking, test preparation, and thinking skills
- Established a communications center to help students improve their oral and written communication skills
- Instituted a first year mentoring program
- Increased cumulative grade point average from 1.6 to 2.4

Academic Affairs

Implemented a series of action steps in Academic Affairs designed to better standardize course content, and promote the development of a more engaging teaching and learning environment.

- Developed learning outcomes and assessment measures for all courses
- Created a master syllabi for all courses
- Developed curriculum maps for all academic programs
- Developed learning outcomes and assessment measures for each program of study
- Increased student and faculty fluency with learning management systems (LMS)
- Established professional develop series designed to increase faculty proficiency of instructional delivery
- Developed and established student advising process that includes mentoring and career development.
- Established course rotations to increase the predictability of course offerings.
- Created a new honors program.
- Redesigned student advising process to ensure successful matriculation
- Created a Math and technology lab
- Established four computer labs on campus for students

DEVELOP A PROCESS LEADING TO FINANCIAL SUSTAINABILITY

- Established and implemented a budget building and management process that has resulted in the end of deficit spending
- Implemented 'Best Practices' in the business office and hired new staff
- Consolidated bank accounts to secure better rates
- Implemented better budget building processes to estimate more precise revenue expenditure projections
- Negotiated several contracts with companies that the college outsources services
- Implemented an energy savings program
- Selected vendors offering more competitive rates
- Developed a more focused and intestinal student recruitment program

IMPROVE THE PHYSICAL PLANT

Established and implemented a deferred maintenance priority list that has resulted in:

- Repaired HVAC systems on campus
- Installed wireless technology throughout the campus
- Repaired all campus roofs to stop water leakage
- Installed distance learning and state of the art video technology in four classrooms and both auditoriums
- Established ten 'Smart' classrooms

Funding for projects came from the appropriate use of federal grants. Many of the trustees were pleasantly surprised with the amount of progress being made in the monthly reports and expressed solid support for President Palmer. They even voted to extend his contract three additional years. However, the chair of the board would not allow President Palmer to run the college without an enormous level of interference. Martin did not like to be micro-managed and saw no need for the interventions given all of the success. The chair would challenge every decision, want to be involved in every aspect of the college, demanded detailed written reports for every move, and called Martin all day, every day. Dr. palmer's leadership style had always called for a great deal of involvement in the decision making process from all sectors of the enterprise. He enjoyed the vetting process and believed that results produced more informed and better decisions. Yet Martin was beginning to dread any conversations with, actually attacks from, the board chair. The board chair had no experience leading any organization. He reminded Martin of a fish out of water when discussing the next steps for the college. The chair wanted to wait even though the step by step process for making change was followed and had been very successful. He was often the only negative vote when seeking board approval. At times it seemed that the chair saw Martin as a competitor. Martin would often remind the chair that this work was not about him as President, but rather was focused on improving the college. In reality the board chair was overwhelmed with the speed of positive change on campus. He told other board members that he never thought this college could improve like this, especially at the current pace. What a shame!

Martin told me that he made a huge mistake when he decided to ignore some of the chair's calls on the weekend and before five in the morning. While he still supported the premise that an engaged group of stakeholders presented the best chances for successful decision making, Martin found himself making fewer and fewer calls to the chair of the board. President Palmer said he made another mistake when he decided to stop the chair from being so involved in the day to day running of the campus. Martin did this to avoid all of the micromanaging attempts from the chair of the board, his negative vibe and to avoid being called insubordinate. This decision caused an even deeper disconnect between Martin and the board chair, his boss. These decisions also began the end of Martin's presidency. Martin was abruptly removed from his position, without a majority vote from the board, just short of his third anniversary despite the huge success of the college during his tenure and extended contract. The chair told a handful of the board members that Martin failed due to low student enrollment. The enrollment plan, approved by the board nearly two years prior to this time, clearly outlined an initial drop in enrollment as the college worked to improve the academic profile of the student body. The chair also sited issues related to accreditation and budget. He even told this small group of trustees that Martin had been insubordinate with him on numerous occasions. All statements were blatant lies and proven to be so just a few months later. The external audit that was finalized just after Martin's departure was the best audit in the recent history of the college. The college ended the fiscal year with a small six figure surplus. The current year was on schedule to end with over a one million dollar surplus. The college was indeed headed for fiscal sustainability. The college had turned the corner and was now positioned to become a good liberal arts institution of higher education. It would need to continue along this path however without Martin.

Martin told me that he moved away from his philosophy of engaged leadership. Dr. Palmer no longer inspired stakeholder participation at the level needed. Martin began to shy away from meaningful discussions, first with the board chair and then with his gang of four, regarding the future of the college. This president no longer exhibited the kind of enthusiasm needed to keep stakeholders actively engaged in their process of change. He had just grown tired of the backwards mentality of the board chair and his gang of four. Martin said that this anchor felt like it was wrapped around his throat, getting tighter each day.

He also said that moving away from engaged leadership was a huge mistake on his part. Martin said that he should have realized that he set himself up to be released by giving up on his relationship with the board chair. He could have employed a much slower process of change, but just could not make himself do it. Martin just hoped that the next president would be able to work better with the board chair and continue to help the college move forward.

Just what was this concept of engaged leadership that Martin kept referring to? How would this form of leadership have made a difference?

CHAPTER 4

A CULTURE OF DEFEAT

When looking deeper into Dr. Palmer's situation, one begins to see that he was working within a way of thinking, believing and acting that was counter to his own. Martin was very familiar to this way of life. It represented the culture of his youth. It is the culture that most of his family back home lives each day. It represented the culture that Martin fought so hard to break through. Dr. Palmer was attempting to work with other individuals to create a teaching and learning environment that would provide a pathway out of this self-defeating way of life for students with the desire to do so. He wanted to be a part of something special. Martin believed that they could help to empower young adults to see a better world and become a part of it. Dr. Palmer called this way of life as a Culture of Defeat.

LOOKING BACK

A child is born. His father, on the eighth day of his life, lifts his son to a starry heavenly night, names him and tells him, "Behold, the only thing greater than yourself." The beginning of life, starting with the realization of who (name) you are and whose (God) you are. The beginning of life built on strong, good, spiritual principles. A way of life built on honoring thy mother and father, treating others with the same dignity and respect you would have them treat you and keeping God first in your life. God bless the child.

Later, a rite of passage into manhood takes place. Becoming a man and eagerly taking on the responsibilities, and privileges, this passage entails – never to go back to the way things once were as a child. This successful rite of passage was expected of all the young men. Expectations were high. A way of life perpetuated through customs passed on each generation. Certain principles and values were a way of life. These customs brought meaning to life. These customs gave each member of the community a better sense of who they were and provided a pathway leading back from which one came... (to the only thing greater than...). This proud traditional way of life continued for a long time, for some. For others, life would drastically change.

This particular young man is seen alone by those who would do him harm. He runs, but is surrounded. He fights, killing one, but there are too many. They put him in shackles, then step back. He continues to fight, to struggle against the chains, to cry out. As he struggles he envisions his parents, family, and friends – his whole world before him and prays to his God that he might see them again. He prays for the warriors to come running to release him from his enemies. He prays for freedom. He fights, and fights, and fights until all energy is drained, until hope begins to wane. He is captured, caged, then packed into a ship, never to see his loved ones or his home again. He is now a slave. His father and other members of their community look for him. They find some of his possessions and realize what has happened. His son will forever be lost to them, in this life.

The middle passage begins. He is packed with many others like sardines in the hull of a ship. They set sail on a nightmare no human should ever experience.

The first order of business for the captors is control. In order to control their "cargo", these proud responsible and spiritually principled people, all that they know and love is systematically taken away. He, and the others, are not allowed to speak in their native tongue, nor practice the traditions that bring them comfort and meaning to their lives. He is later given a new name and punished for using his birth name given by his father. He is told that, and treated, as though he were only one step above an animal. He is taken away from all he knows and loves, and told untruths about himself and his new world. All of the tactics are designed to confuse and therefore control. He is no longer called a man, a proud African man of the Mandingo, Fulani, Ibo, Asante, Holof, or Ewe. He is now called a savage, jungle bunny, jigaboo, saucer lips, spear chucker, Negro, nega, or lazy nigger. He is a slave in America.

These acts, designed to control the slave, continue to play a major role in how we relate to one another.

To make a black African a slave, white America chose to destroy the black family unit. Human rights, such as marriages, family privileges parents and child relationships, were taken from blacks. Blacks were not considered human beings. The buying and selling of slaves was as common as the buying and selling of horses and cattle. Family members were separated. Many never saw each other again. The great freedoms that the early white fathers of America fought and stood for were not applied to the black family (Williams, 1990, p. 9).

CONTROL

In a patriarchal society, one with the man as head, leadership is destroyed when the head is chopped off – or at least out of contact with the rest of the body. This ideology has developed into a tool often employed during and after slavery. During slavery, the male slave could not protect his family. His wife, with marriage for slaves not even sanctioned by the white society, could be taken as a concubine or belly warmer at any time. Her slave master or son or overseer – or one of the master's friends often took her for pleasurable entertainment. Sometimes she was used with another African slave for studding purposes. Either way the master benefited with the birthing of new slaves. The man's children could and often were taken and sold. He was never called mister or treated anything close to any white man.

After slavery, the opportunities to own land and receive a quality education were short lived. Both legal (Jim Crow/Black Codes) and illegal (KKK) efforts were employed to prevent equality of opportunities for the freed slave. Low paying jobs, if any, poor treatment at the job, no prospects for advancement and a continuous barrage of negative messages worked t diminish the hopes of black men. The reactions are one of complacency (drunkenness/yessa man) or anger (prison/early death). Both actions, and results, take the role of leadership out of the black man's hands. Often black women were afforded slightly better opportunities than their male counterparts, thus weakening the chances for male leadership in the home. Inferiority sets in, in the minds of both the oppressor and the oppressed.

For several centuries white America has tried to develop concepts of blacks as being inferior, and also to promote concepts of whites as being superior. Consequently, all Americans have been affected by these slavery concepts. When the average white person, sees a black person, the white person's self-esteem and self-worth automatically go up. It does not matter whether the white person is tall, short, skinny, fat, stupid, wise, or otherwise, his or her concept of superiority is reinforced. Whenever a black person sees a white person his or her concept of inferiority is reinforced. These feelings are automatic unless an aggressive effort has been made to counter thee impressions. Why are these feelings automatic? They are such because of the slavery experience in America and the constant and continues perpetuation of concepts of slavery (William, 1990, p. 75).

QUESTIONS AND SOME ANSWERS

1. Why has there been such a strong need to stereotype then segregate people into groups?
2. What effects do these varying designations have on peoples' lives?
3. Who determines where someone else fits (race, sexual orientation, religious affiliations, social economic status, etc. designation)?
4. How has this system of categorization helped to direct life pathways chosen by or imposed upon the majority of Negroes, Coloreds, Blacks, Afro-Americans – African Americans, and others?
5. When did "The only thing greater than you" become other people?

In the book "Killers of the Dream," Lillian Smith tells the reader about a significant event in her life as a young girl. This event helped to shape her thinking for many years. In this true story a little white girl is found living with an older black couple in the colored section of town. The white women's club becomes so enraged by the fact that a little white girl was living, in such deplorable conditions, with black people in colored town that they force the sheriff to take the little girl from them. The little girl moves in with Lillian and her family. She demonstrates high levels of achievement in school and begins to fit into her new family just fine. Subsequent investigations reveal that the little white girl is actually a product of a rape that occurred between her black mother and rapist white father. The little white girl, in their eyes, is actually a little black girl. At this point it was agreed that she would be returned to the elderly black couple who happened to be her grandparents in the morning. Lillian, a little white girl of privilege, does not understand what has happened. She could not understand why they took her new little sister away from her. After some discussion with her parents, and a great deal of crying, these thoughts solidify in Lillian's young mind.

But I felt compelled to believe they (her parents) were right. It was the only way my world could be held together. And, slowly, it began to seep through me: I was white. She was colored. We must not be together. Though you ate with your nurse when you were little, it was bad to eat with any colored person after that. It was bad just as other things were bad that your mother had told you. It was bad that she was to sleep in the room with me that night. It was bad (Smith, 1961, p. 38).

This system of categorization has, for many, created a foundation of thought about African Americans. This system of reinforced subliminal messages and preconceived notions created by a series of propagandized stories addressing the academic, social, political and physical attributes or lack thereof of African Americans continues to grow and perpetuate itself. For example: In order to keep a person in his place you must find a way to make him accept his lot in life. Cultural genocide became the primary strategy. Slave masters and others in our society went to great lengths to systematically strip African slaves of their cultural foundations, then create a new set of negative beliefs in its place. We believe this is part of the system that allowed slavery to exist for so long in this country. A system that caused many of our ancestors to believe the African slave to be sub-human, second-rate and unable to take adequate care of himself without help. (Kind of reminds one of today's ultra-liberals?) It is the system of beliefs that supported or failed to fight aggressively against Jim Crow. How else could one human being not treat another with the same kind of dignity and respect they expect? (Is this how Californians and others are looking at illegal and legal immigrants from south of the border these days?) More recently, the Anti-Affirmative Action movement is rooted in this same soil of misinformation and propaganda. Arguments seem to focus on the assumed abilities of one group of people versus another instead of addressing the need for equal opportunities. Take a moment to think about how most individuals would answer the following questionnaire.

Thinking About Privilege, Power and Difference
(adapted by Cornell Thomas from Johnson, 2001)

Please check the answer under each question that best reflects your current thinking.

1. _____ would be less likely to be arrested; once arrested, less likely to be convicted and, once convicted, less likely to go to prison, regardless of the crime or circumstances. Please fill in the blank with one the groups listed below.

   Blacks
   Hispanics
   Whites
   Asians

2. _____ can succeed without others' being surprised. Please fill in the blank with one of the groups listed below.

   Female
   Male

3. _____ can usually assume that national heroes, success models, and other figures held up for general admiration will be of their race. Please fill in the blank with one of the groups listed below.

   Blacks
   Hispanics
   Whites
   Asians

4. _____ are more likely to be given early opportunities to show what they can do at work, to be identified as potential candidates for promotion, to be mentored, to be given a second chance when they fail, and to be allowed to treat failure as a learning experience rather than as an indication of who they are and the shortcomings of their gender. Please fill in the blank with one of the groups listed below.

   Females
   Males

5. _____ don't have to deal with an endless and exhausting stream of attention to their race. They simply take their race for granted as unremarkable to the extent of experiencing themselves as not even having a race. Please fill in the blank with one of the groups listed below.

   Blacks
   Hispanics
   Whites
   Asians

6. _____ can generally assume that when they go out in public, they won't be sexually harassed or assaulted, and if they are victimized, they won't be asked to explain what they were doing there. Please fill in the blank with one of the groups listed below.

   Females
   Males

7. Because privileged groups are assumed to represent society as a whole, "American," for example, is culturally defined as _____, in spite of the diversity of the population. You can see this in a statement like, "Americans must learn to be more tolerant of other races." Please fill in the blank with one of the groups listed below.

   Blacks
   Hispanics
   Whites
   Asians

8. _____ have greater access to quality education and health care. Please fill in the blank with one of the groups listed below.

   Blacks
   Hispanics
   Whites
   Asians

9. In most professions and upper-level occupations, men/women are held to a lower standard than men/women. Circle men or women to answer this statement.

   _____ representation in government and the ruling circles of corporations, universities, and other organizations is disproportionately high. Please fill in the blank with one of the groups listed below.

   Blacks
   Hispanics
   Whites
   Asians

10. _____ representation in government and the ruling circles of corporations, universities, and other organizations is disproportionately high. Please fill in the blank with one of the groups listed below.

    Females
    Males

11. _____ children are more likely to come from families that see the 'fine arts' as part of the process of becoming well-educated and culturally competent individuals. Please fill in the blank with one of the groups listed below.

Low WIncome
Middle Income
High Income

12. _____ children are more likely to have adults in their lives that demonstrate how to become 'successful' in our society. Please fill in the blank with one of the groups listed below.

Low Income
Middle Income
High Income

13. Children from low income families have difficulty transitioning to our school primarily due to:

A lack of support from their parents
A lack of enrichment experiences outside of school
Lower levels of intelligence
A society that tells us, and them, the they are academically inferior
All of the above

14. _____ children have greater access to quality education and health care. Please fill in the blank with one of the groups listed below.

Low Income
Middle Income
High Income

Children from low income families seem to lack self-esteem at our school because:

- They have not traveled like our other students.
- They lack the appropriate clothing for social events.
- Their parents don't seem to be as sophisticated and/or educated as other student's parents.
- The other students live in much bigger and better homes and neighborhoods.
- All of the above.

Children from low income families are successful at our school when they:

- Embrace the values that we support
- Are challenged academically just like all of our students
- Are assigned an upper class-person as a student mentor
- When we find ways to embrace the values they bring to the school
- All of the above

The challenges of privilege, power and difference in our society should be addressed by:

• The group challenging the status quo
• The privileged group
• All of us

Particular to this discussion and questionnaire, this system of beliefs continues to provide justification for the unequal educational opportunities existing in our society and therefore schools. Dr. Palmer, members of his new leadership team, some trustees, faculty, staff, students and community leaders believed that they could uncloak these actions and create new pathways moving from a culture of defeat to a culture of success on this campus.

Uncloaking

Star Trek fans are very familiar with the cloaking device. So are many others. The Klingons, once an arch enemy of the Federation, would cloak their starships in order to gain a strategic advantage over their enemies before attacking. However, in order to fire upon their enemies Klingons were required to uncloak, become visible for all to see. Over time the Federation starships began to find ways to detect Klingon starships even while they were cloaked. Once uncloaked all could clearly see the challenges before them and take action to successfully meet that challenge.

Often issues of inequality and discrimination are cloaked. Inequality and discrimination are often cloaked with descriptions of difference among and between human beings as 'less than'. For example, women are described as the weaker sex, gays as the devil's own and minorities as...well, minor.

These well developed and internalized socially constructed beliefs inform our thinking and guide our actions. Regarding differences in this way provides the justification needed for some of us to treat one human being better than another. It also cloaks the truth. At the same time these ways of differentiating human beings creates pathways of life full of steep hills, slippery slopes and seemingly insurmountable barriers for many individuals in our world. All because of a socially constructed way of life that provides privileges for an 'elite' few while vilifying others.

Instead, one of the overarching goals of our society must bring focused attention to issues of diversity and privilege. This work is designed in a variety of ways to empower learners to think about and better understand differences using a broader and more multidimensional lens. The premise supporting this work believes that equality and justice for all will take the place of privilege and discrimination when notions of differences as 'less than' are demystified, debunked, and uncloaked for what they really are. This work is guided by the need to broaden the perspective of learners in order to uncloak these socially constructed, negative images regarding differences. And are further guided by three concepts regarding differences and our commitment to eradicate the injustices (privilege) that permeate the very core of our society: Identity – Presence – Intentionality. Historical facts provide true credit (identity) to those individuals and groups that were instrumental in the development of this great nation. These facts and the connecting perspectives have often been forgotten or ignored (cloaked) in mainstream discussions. Sharing our true history and the contributions of all individuals would help to obliterate the false and negative thoughts that current exist and create a new and truer appreciation for the people (presence) who are a part of our society and beyond.

These new and corrected perspectives and experiences, once accepted and internalized, will also lead to a change in how we live our lives. The structure and experiences provided from a focus on these new and corrected perspectives and experiences will cause most, if not all, learners to work towards social change (intentionality). The social change referred to here empowers us to diminish the negative impact of current notions regarding difference. This focus will also help us to value tradition, better understand the evolution of traditions, and embrace our role in making this change a positive process for all. This work will help learners become more intentional in their own work. These are the actions that most, if not all of us, want to see accomplished.

An inclusive community of learners actively seeks to bring clarity to differences (identity) in positive ways. Inclusion calls for these identities to have a voice (presence) in what the collective of voices is becoming as a community. Active participation (intentionality) then becomes the engine that can and will change the world.

Engaged leaders make this premise a focal point in their work. Creating an environment that reinforces engaged and active involvement helps to empower individuals to develop a more internalized understanding of issues being discussed. This process often touches the heart of the learner. A process that moves the learner from seeking 'the answer' to seeking personal meaning is one worthy of our consideration and use. This process will help all of us help change the world in positive and productive ways. This process does indeed provide a path that leads us in this work to uncloak issues of inequality and discrimination. Changing how we engage all members of an organization, a school for example, in this way will produce new advocates committed to the eradication of the injustices (privilege) that community permeates the core of our society. Positive change initiatives will then occur.

MOVING FORWARD

"Foundation" implies a single, firm, enduring, and fixed base on which to build our ideas and practices as educators. It implies a base of shared meanings about what knowledge is worth teaching and how it should be taught. The assumption is that educators have agreed, or can be convinced to agree, to share these founding meanings because they have some basis in "fact" and "reality" (Ellsworth, 1994, p. 103).

What if there was some way to build a new foundation of thoughts? How could we take, for instance, the story of enslavement (Looking Back) and use it as a guiding rod toward empowerment for positive academic, social, political and physical growth? The story might continue by saying:

Despite all the attempts to put and keep the enslaved African down, despite attempts to destroy his very soul, work toward freedom continued. Each year more and more slaves found routes to freedom. Other slaves found ways to worship and secure some form of education. Many white men and women did not believe the propaganda generated to vilify the enslaved and grew more powerful in their fight against slavery. They finally won this battle in 1865.

After slavery, with the fight for freedom won, battle lines for equality were quickly drawn. Each year more former slaves learned to read and write. More former slaves learned, although in very tiny steps, how to secure a better future for themselves and their children. Because of his spiritual self and belief in his God, the now freed slave persevered through such atrocities as Jim Crow and vigilante group actions. The freed slave kept his eyes on the prize and worked hard for he indeed had faith in knowing there would be better days to come. He began to define for himself a new identity. This new identity was rooted once again in the past. A past built on a foundation starting with the realization of who you are and whose you are. A foundation of life built on strong, good, spiritual principles. Hope and faith were rekindled!

One's basic identity is one's self-identity, which is ultimately one's cultural identity; without a strong cultural identity, one is lost. Black children do not know their people's story and white children do not know the story, but remembrance is a vital requisite for understanding and humility... Without an understanding of the historical experiences of African people, American children cannot make any real headway in addressing the problems of the present (Asante, 1991, p. 177).

Our history speaks of the trials, tribulations and triumphs during and after slavery in this country. There is indeed much work still to be done. We can however find links to our past that will propel us forward. The triumphs need more emphasis. We must look back (Sankofa) in order to move forward. Teachers drawing from past experiences of triumph over pain can create in their classrooms a powerful sense of hope. With hope comes work; with work comes accomplishment; and with accomplishment comes success. Looking at how far the once enslaved African has come in this country and how this has been accomplished can be the energy needed to triple the output in a very short period of time. Is this not what we want to see achieved by all students? If yes is our answer, we must begin to draw on this history, and on the personal stories of the children in our classrooms, to promote a very powerful message. A message of hope and faith; of respecting the past and valuing each student's abilities becomes a classroom culture destined for greatness.

Think of how empowered young African Americans (and others using a similar process) might feel to see their stories connected to the fight for freedom, just like those so eloquently described throughout our history for white America?

They would begin to see themselves as contributors to the greatness of this nation instead of parasites needing to be continuously helped, and controlled. Continue this train of thoughts with us, we submit to you that for teachers:

Factors for success in classrooms, relationships built on a foundation of trust, respect, valuing and caring, would be more prevalent between teachers and students in our schools. For example, instead of focusing on current 'at risk' issues from a pathological reference point, we would, because of past contributions, be able to ignore much of the remaining propaganda, the subliminal messages bombarding us each day of our lives, see potential a better tomorrow in all of our students.

Teachers would be willing and able to find more ways to connect what we want students to know with what they already know. We would begin to see more value in what knowledge students bring with them to school. We would be focused on the positive potential of the students we teach.

More teachers would begin to realize the gifts of each student.

We would begin to see more real student centered teaching and learning activities in all classrooms. These activities seem to occur more frequently when teachers believe in the student's ability and desire to learn. When teachers believe in the abilities of their students, they are more willing to empower students to begin the process of learning how to learn for themselves. These sets of beliefs must help form this new proposed foundation of thought.

More students would be made aware of their ability to modify and even play a major role in reconstructing the social environment. They become active, instead of passive members of society.

There would be more focus on the premise that students learn how to learn due to emphasis placed on internalizing experiences and the teacher's demonstrated belief in student capital.

CONCLUDING THOUGHTS

We do not really see through our eyes or hear through our ears, but through our beliefs. To put our beliefs on hold is to cease to exist as ourselves for a moment – and that is not easy. It is painful as well, because it means turning yourself inside out, giving up your own sense of who you are, and being willing to see yourself in the unflattering light of another's angry gaze. It is not easy, but it is the only way to learn what it might feel like to be someone else and the only way to start the dialogue (Delpit, 1998, p. 297).

When teachers begin to see the potential power in their positions and accept challenges instead of seeing problems then positive change will occur. In these settings students try harder primarily due to a developing thirst and desire to explore the unknown in an environment that sees learning as an adventure.

A good beginning to this process is for teachers to begin to value what students bring to school and share our history as an empowering message. Teachers find ways to connect the knowledge we want students to internalize with information they already know and with history, our true history. We no longer ignore their life experiences and the triumphs of all our ancestors. Our goal is to connect new learning with existing knowledge and truth thus building upon a foundation of strength, familiarity, honesty and empowerment.

For students it is a way to internalize information. By connecting new learning with existing knowledge and including personal historical facts, students are more successful at constructing their own relational bridges as a way of remembering new learning and bringing new meanings to old knowledge. In other words, students become empowered. They begin to understand the responsibilities and commitments weaved into the very fabric of its meaning, thus reinforcing and bringing positive meaning to self-empowerment. Empowered students described here also begin to enjoy both the work and even more the resulting benefits to their lives. They know how and want to succeed. The enemy outside is now defeated by the self within.

And I saw a new heaven and new earth, for the first heaven and the first earth were passed away . . . And I heard a great voice out of heaven saying, Behold..., I make all things new (Revelation: 21)

REFERENCES

Asante, M. (1991). The Afrocentric Idea in Education. The Journal of Negro Education, 60, no.2.
Delpit, L. (1988). The Silenced Dialogue: Power and Pedagogy in Educating Other People's Children. Harvard Educational Review, Vol.58, No.3, 280–298.
Diop, C. (1974). The African Origin of Civilization: Myth or Reality.Chicago: Lawrence Hill Books.
Ellsworth, E. (1994). Representation, Self-Representation, and the Meanings of Difference: Questions for Educators. In Martusewicz, R. & Reynolds, W. (Eds.) Inside Out: Contemporary Critical Perspectives in Education. New York: St. Martin's Press.
Hilliard, A. (1995). The Maroon Within Us. Baltimore: Black Classic Press.
Hord, F. and Lee, J. (Eds.) (1995). I Am Because We Are: Readings in Black Philosophy. Boston: University of Massachusetts Press.
Smith, L. (1961) Killers of the Dream. New York: Norton & Company.
Williams, R. (1990). They Stole It But You Must Return It. Rochester, New York:HRMA Publishing.
Woodson, C. (1933). The Mis-Education of the Negro. Washington, DC: Associated Publishers.

CHAPTER 5

A CULTURE OF POSSIBILITIES

A call for the engaged leader was presented in a previous chapter. In that chapter the engaged leader was described as a person who inspires participation, encourages meaningful work relationships between stakeholders, and is enthusiastic about the possibilities that emerge from this type of dynamic, interactive, inclusive process.

I went on to describe the engaged leader as one who works to include the voices of all stakeholders as the organization (school) works to accomplish stated goals. The engaged leader is an advocate of empowerment. The engaged leader helps to create the kind of teaching and learning environment that causes others to critically examine their own priorities, abilities and perspectives. It is the kind of environment that causes individuals to continually improve their work, and challenge and help other stakeholders to do the same. Much of the success of this work depends on the ability to connect with others in meaningful conversations and actions.

The national movement to evaluate the success of teaching and learning in public schools had curtailed the growth of collaboratively engaged and inclusive organizational environments. This movement has hindered the ultimate goal of our educational system: helping to empower learners to learn how to learn for themselves. High stakes testing continues to promote memorization and rote learning, at best. The future of students is unfairly impacted in this environment of high stakes testing. High stakes testing continues to promote rote learning, resulting in the temporary memorization of information for most. Often memorized information has little to no depth of understanding or connection to important aspects of student's lives. Students experiencing teaching and learning in these settings are seldom able to move beyond true or false and right or wrong statements. While most students are taught in a black and white world of either – or, they are asked to live in the multiple colors that exist in between black and white, with little to no preparation. They develop limited abilities to address 'why'; think about the 'what ifs'; to elaborate on topics being addressed; and demonstrate a lack of ability to create new ways of thinking and conceptualizing the world around them. In other words, learning to think critically and freely about issues is not adequately addressed.

I am not promoting any type of conspiracy theory to limit access to the *American Dream* for some in our society. However one wonders, how can anyone support the results of a high stakes testing program that is creating a more tiered society within our country. After-all, most, if not all, quality private schools understand the importance of empowering students to think and learn for themselves. They know, and their actions support, that future leaders must be prepared to matriculate through college. Graduates must have the ability to develop new ways of thinking and living, continue to create new technologies, and motivate others, from all walks of life, to work with them. High stakes testing has resulted in a high number of learners in these environments dropping out of school, filling our prison systems, lengthening our unemployment lines, and adding to the welfare numbers. Our system of high stakes testing is creating citizens with limited options before them and lacking the ability to think critically about issues that have the potential to improve their lot in life. Many of the jobs requiring high levels of thinking, creativity and leadership are being secured by individuals graduating from our private schools, or from other countries. These results just cannot be part of a plan that enhances the future of our county, right? Yet high stakes testing continues along this path of disastrous results. One can only wonder, why? High stakes testing has become another gate keeper, convincing most students that they are not prepared for higher levels of learning, or full membership in our society.

The process of high stakes testing is also tied to the evaluation of teacher performance in many public school districts. Often included is the over-all evaluative performance of each school, and its leadership. Educator's jobs are often on the line. The impact of these rules has seen more cases of testing fraud as high stakes testing has spread across the nation. Teachers and administrators have been accused, and many times, prosecuted for infractions such as:

- falsifying student test scores,
- making sure that certain students are marked absent during testing periods,
- securing advance copies of the test,
- promoting students to avoid testing, and
- finding ways that allow students to cheat on these test.

These and other unethical activities have taken place as a way to avoid embarrassing reports that are shared with the public and, in some cases, to ensure pay raises and avoid loss of employment. Some teachers have simply reverted to just teaching to the test, over and over again. The true purpose of teaching and learning has been lost in many of our public schools. Our students are not being prepared to maximize their capacity to learn.

District ratings also have an economic impact on the city and area communities. Ratings of school districts, based primarily on high stakes test scores, have become an important evaluative measure when corporations consider relocation and/or expansion. Parents often consider this data when selecting where they choose to live and raise their families.

It seems that those supporting high stakes testing have either lowered their expectations of most students attending public schools, are misguided when it comes to how and when learning occurs best, are purposely guaranteeing a workforce of followers and high unemployment, or all of the above. Either way, engaged leaders must lead a process that moves us away from this way of teaching and learning, and still achieve high levels of academic success. High stakes testing has joined other standardized test, SAT, ACT, GRE, GMAT, MCAT, etc. to unfairly limit the number of individuals seeking to improve their lives through a quality education.

One of the most important elements within an educational culture of possibilities is a focus on connecting. Connecting with others and ourselves provides the bridge needed to connect internalized understandings, knowledge, with new information. Connecting in this way helps us to internalize, and therefore learn, new information. Connecting in this way represents a better teaching and learning process than the techniques utilized in support of high stakes testing.

Engaged pedagogical practices are utilized by excellent teachers in many school settings. These teachers embrace the premise that students learn best when they are actively engaged in the teaching and learning process. It is important here to realize that both students and teachers are learners in this type of learning environment. Teachers utilizing engaged pedagogical methodology believe that the knowledge each student brings with them is essential to the internalization of the new information that they want learners to learn. Connecting, bridging between what students already know with information the teachers wants them to learn, becomes a major point of focus and action. In these settings all are teachers and all are learners. All participants make valuable contributions to the teaching and learning process and all voices are very important.

A great way for teachers to connect with students is during guided practice sessions. Most lesson cycles provide students with opportunities to practice what was just taught. This time is often called guided practice. During guided practice the teacher works the room, stopping by each student to see if they are successfully understanding the concepts that have recently been taught. Guided practice sessions offer great opportunities for teachers to connect existing knowledge with new information and new ways to think about something. Similar techniques are employed by the engaged leader.

Engaged leaders use this process of connecting to bridge existing knowledge of the mission, vision and action steps of the organization with the changes needed for continued success. This process helps to bring clarity where the organization currently stands, the need to address real and potential shortfalls, and the action steps to move forward in successful ways. Change is often met with opposition by stakeholders, primarily due to perceived negatives, what I am calling perceptual barriers. Much of the opposition and perceptual barriers are caused by a lack of vision regarding the future. Often stakeholders become concerned about their role in the organization and how that role will be changed, or eliminated. Prior experience with organizational change fuels these kind of concerns. They often refer to organizational change that resulted in downsizing, the call for new sets of skills and abilities, a diminishing value of their previous contributions to the organization. These perceptual barriers to change can be improved when more clarity of the purpose and proposed results can be shared early and throughout the process. Connecting becomes the pathway facilitating the changes that need to occur.

One such way to accomplish a better change process is through a 'straw-person' approach. This straw-person approach is made up of several key steps. We will provide a general outline here. The Engaged Leader begins this approach with a series of small group discussions within every unit/department of the organization. These discussions should begin with an overview of the organization focused on its perceived strengths, weakness, opportunities and threats. A generalized vision of the future of the organization should also be shared. The ensuing discussions should then focus on framing and refining the vision of the future and the potential action steps needed to accomplish said goals. Each of these discussions should end with a written response from the leader that capsulized all that was said and accomplished. All of these written responses should be shared on a website designated to document and share the process of change and is available for all stakeholders to review and make comments. The key for success of this initiative is the sharing of tentative goals, throughout the entire process of refinement that is inclusive of all stakeholders who choose to engage. All stakeholders should have the ability to provide their own thoughts, without reprisal, throughout the process.

Unit/department leaders and key stakeholders, as identified by each group of stakeholders, should then meet to review all input and develop a position paper to bring clarity and direction to the establishment, or to reaffirm the existing, mission, vision and action steps needed to move forward. This straw-person document is then used to conduct a series of SWOT analysis sessions scheduled by units/department and additional sessions open to all stakeholders. A SWOT or SLOT analysis is part of some strategic planning processes. It is used as an evaluative tool designed to identify the strengths within organizations and those attributes that can be utilized for strategic advantage. The process also helps individuals identify the weaknesses and/or limitations within the organization. Opportunities to improve performance and outcomes emerge. In addition, potential and real threats are exposed before more harm is done. The SWOT sessions should all begin, using skilled facilitators, with each person framing their reactions in writing to the straw-person document. During the next step individuals move into small groups of no more than five to discuss and refine their thoughts. This step is followed by the actual SWOT process with the entire group. These interim steps help to encourage and hear the voices of all participants. It helps to avoid the often occurrence of dominate voices only being heard. The results of each session is then included on the website for all to review, discuss, and make comments.

The unit/department leaders and key stakeholder group then reviews each document to refine the straw-person document once again. Of critical importance throughout this process is the emphasis placed on outcomes. These outcomes help all stakeholders identify their roles in the organization as it evolves/changes. Sometimes this process will help some individuals see the need to separate from the organization when they have a disconnection with the new direction.

A series of presentations to stakeholders by the engaged leader should then take place. The presentations should be designed to bring clarity to the set of action steps that have emerged to address the proposed revisions. It is very important that each member of the organization sees their role. Therefore each presentation will be somewhat different, based on the unit/department being addressed. Again, the presentations help each person envision their role in this process of change. They can also help to finalize the process with their thoughts and comments.

After some time for reflection, discussion, and possible refinements, a celebration to launch the change process takes place as the move forward begins. Scheduled updates and a process for continued assessment and refinement is structured within the change process.

The engaged leader actively works to connect the goals of the organization with the knowledge base and personal realities of each stakeholder as part of the strategic planning and continuation process. The engaged leader makes and maintains individual connections with all direct reports and key stakeholders. She/he charges these individuals to make similar connections with their direct reports and key constituents. The goal of developing and maintaining these types of connections is to make sure, as best we can, that the goals of the organization remain the primary focus. Individual needs are wed to organizational goals in ways that create an environment that Glickman describes as a cause beyond self. The needs of the many (in this case the organization) outweigh the needs of the few, or the one.

For example, a question has emerged from several sectors of the college regarding student enrollment during the annual self-assessment of the strategic plan. Some stakeholders point to diminishing state and federal revenue streams as the reason to make the decision to increase student enrollment by at least ten percent next year. Other stakeholders feel that an additional five hundred students (the ten percent) would create a number of challenges. These challenges would offset the additional revenue generated by these additional students. The additional students would cause some classroom overcrowding, long lines in the food centers, triple beds in residence halls that were specifically designed for two, and high levels of stress and dissatisfaction from all sectors. It was also believed that standards would need to be lowered in order to achieve this ten percent increase in one year. Despite these concerns, supporters for the enrollment increase proposal see it as the best way to address the pending state and federal revenue shortfalls. They also express concern for potential layoffs as a way to counter these projected budget shortfalls. Those opposed to the ten percent increase in student enrollment believe that overcrowding will change the culture of the college, stretch resident hall staff much too thin, and limit direct contact between student and faculty members. Most of those supporting the increase in enrollment represent the ranks of staff members. The majority of those opposing this proposal to increase enrollment represent the ranks of the faculty.

The engaged leader, and leadership team must find ways to bring clarity to the situation, squash rumors, and provide options that most, if not all, stakeholders can embrace. What would you, as an engaged leader, do? Here is one way to address these concerns:

A series of discussions regarding the strengths, weaknesses, opportunities and threats of each position would occur. Leadership would then develop one or more straw person scenarios to be vetted by those actively involved in the process.

Each session would follow a similar series of steps:

1. Each session would begin with an overview of the challenges.
2. After some review and reflection, a generalized vision of projected outcomes, a straw person proposal, would be shared.
3. Each individual would be asked to write down their own reactions to the straw person proposals.
4. Small groups would then be established where reactions to the straw person proposal would be discussed and refined.
5. Responses from each small group would be posted on a dedicated website for all to review.
6. The same process that took place in small groups would then occur with the larger group exploring each small group reaction and working to develop one draft document.
7. A leadership team would take all of this information to modify the straw person proposal.
8. The final step would consist of reaching consensus and a final document to direct next steps.

This process offers everyone with the opportunity to connect their personal concerns and realities with organizational challenges and goals. The process helps to empower each person to wed personal and organizational goals. It also allows for a clearer pathway for the organization to move forward. Of course there are often outliers at times. However, the process creates a better environment of engagement and inclusion. It also improves the organization's chances for success.

Please remember that this overview provides just a generalized outline of this change process. Each organization will find the need to modify this work based on the input and reactions of stakeholders. The key for the engaged leader is to create and maintain as transparent process as possible. The engaged leader must strive to maintain an environment that remains open to all input from stakeholders. The engaged leader must be dedicated to the establishment of an organization that is as transparent as possible, inclusive, and flexible. This kind of environment will energize stakeholders and create the kind of synergy that maximizes the talents and skills of all. The Culture of Possibilities will lead the organization to very high levels of success.

REFERENCES

Burns, J.M. (1978). Leadership. New York: Harper & Row.
Cawelti, G. (1994). Behavior Patterns of Effective Principals. Educational Leadership, 42. 3.
DePree, M. (1990). Leadership is an Art. New York: Crown Publishing.
Edmonds, R. (1979). Effective schools for the urban poor. Educational Leadership, *37*, 15–24.

Hoy, W. and Miskel, C. (1996). Educational Administration: Theory Research and Practice. New York: McGraw-Hill, Inc.

Leithwood, K. (February 1992). "The Move Toward Transformational Leadership." Educational Leadership, pp. 8–12.

Lipham, J. (1981). Effective principal, effective school. National Association of Secondary School Principals Bulletin.

Shulman, L. (2002). Making Differences: A Table of Learning. Change, 34, 36–45.

Spring, J. (1994). Wheels In The Head. New York: McGraw-Hill

CHAPTER 6

ENGAGED LEADERSHIP

A Cultural Perspective

INTRODUCTION

Is Democracy (Inclusion) Another Dream Deferred?

I pledge allegiance to the flag … .

to the republic for which it stands,

one nation … indivisible….

liberty and justice for all.

The Pledge of Allegiance speaks to the premise of Democracy within which our great nation has roots deeply embedded. This premise, when true, causes one to believe that they have the opportunities to dream great dreams and turn them into reality. Yet so many dreams never become reality; so many dreams become nightmares; so many thoughts of the future are now considered by many individuals as mere pipe dreams long forgotten; so many dreams unfulfilled have left turbulent waves of despair; so many dreams unrealized have destroyed families; so many dreams have become living nightmares. Instead of a wheel of fortune, with all positive options, many find themselves spinning the wheel of misfortune, where every stop spells some level of disaster. Most, if not all of us, know of too many people who are spinning this wheel of misfortune, living some version of Langston Hughes' "A Dream Deferred."

What happens to a dream deferred?

Does it dry up

Like a raisin in the sun/

Or fester like a sore –

And then run?

Or crust and sugar over –

Like a syrupy sweet?

Maybe it just sags

Like a heavy load.

Or does it explode?

Those making attempts to describe the United States as the land of opportunity must not know and talk with the same people as I do. They seem to ignore the fact that not everyone has a smooth, clean and clear pathway to the future paved right in front of them. Some roads are full of potholes, steep hills, cloaked cliffs, and huge barriers. For some, the road does not even exist. Why is this still so? We can elect a president considered to be a member of the African-American sector in this country. We now have women running fortune one hundred companies. The Supreme Court is more gender and racially diverse than in any time in our history. Yet is this mere symbolism? Do these stories of success represent mere accommodations? Has the pathway of self determination been cleared? When looking closely at the academic success of students in our public school, it is clear that we will soon see even more barriers towards the pursuit of the American Dream. A true democracy calls for an educated populous. The level of dialogue, the give and take of debates, and the willingness to listen and compromise, require thoughtful folk. Yet the type of engaged and inclusive teaching and learning supporting a true democracy does not exist in most of our public school settings. One wonders why? Educating the next generation of citizens is an essential step towards true democracy (inclusion), with liberty and justice for all.

Parker Palmer provides clarity to this notion of Democracy (Inclusion):

When we choose to engage, not evade, the tension of our differences, we will become better equipped to participate in a government of, by, and for the people as we expand some of our key civic capacities:

- To listen to each other openly and without fear, learning how much we have in common despite our differences
- To deepen our empathy for the alien "other" as we enter imaginatively into the experiences of people whose lives are radically unlike our own
- To hold what we believe and know with conviction and be willing to listen openly to other viewpoints, changing our minds if needed
- To seek out alternative facts and explanations whenever we find reason to doubt our own truth claims or the claims made by others, thus becoming better informed
- To probe, question, explore, and engage in dialogue, developing a fuller, more three-dimensional view of reality in the process
- To enter the conflicted arena of politics, able to hold the dynamics of that complex force field in ways that unite the civic community and empower us to hold government accountable to the will of the people
- To welcome opportunities to participate in collective problem solving and decision making, generating better solutions and making better decisions as we work with competing ideas
- To feel more at home on the face of the earth amid differences of many sorts, better able to enjoy the fruits of diversity (Palmer, 2011, pp. 14–15).

As we broaden this look more globally, how are the changing dynamics in the world impacting our actions towards a true democracy? And do these shifts, primarily economic in nature; represent the engine that will really lead to the change we seek? Well, let's explore these issues as we ponder the question: Is Democracy (Inclusion) another Dream Deferred?

DISCUSSION

> … if inequity has been institutionalized in the theories, norms, and practices of our society, and if researchers and administrators reify inequity and injustice by failing to examine, question, and redress the inequities they see, then there is much to be done. Larson, C. & Murtadha, K. (2003), p. 134.

Premises provide a starting point for thinking about and acting on an idea or concept. These concepts often represent the foundation upon which a person lives their life. Premises help to form an individual's foundation; culture; their way of thinking and living. Presented here is the premise that there are institutionalized beliefs and practices within schools about students, parents, our society, and the educator's responsibilities to the learner that must be re-examined, and changed. This premise is based on the belief that most, if not all, educators want to be a part of highly successful teaching and learning environments and that this is indeed the goal of school leaders. A major area to be addressed here is how we better understand the students that we teach and developing a better understanding of why we think and act the way that we do.

Educational leaders are expected to develop learning communities, build the professional capacity of teachers, take advice from parents, engage in collaborative and consultative decision making, resolve conflicts, engage in effective instructional leadership, and attend respectfully, immediately, and appropriately to the needs and requests of families with diverse cultural, ethnic, and socioeconomic backgrounds. Shields (2004), p. 109.

Inequity has indeed been institutionalized in just about every aspect of our lives. In other words, the way we think about ourselves and other individuals has been framed by a set of societal norms purposely designed to think that different means less than. The answers to the questionnaire below, if given honestly, will confirm this statement.

THINKING ABOUT CULTURE QUESTIONNAIRE

Please fill each blank with the name of a group that you have heard about.

1. _____ are more likely to listen to rap music.

2. _____ can usually assume that national heroes, successful political and business leaders and other figures held up for general admiration will be representative of their group.

3. _____ are more likely to drop out of high school.

4. _____ are more likely to have a baby as a teenager.

5. _____ are more likely to rob a small convenience store.

6. _____ are more likely to cheat on their taxes.

7. _____ are more likely to be given early opportunities to show what they can do at work.

8. _____ are more likely to prefer multiple sex partners.

9. _____ are more likely to be considered athletes on campus.

10. _____ are more likely to become president of the United States.

11. _____ is less likely to worry about the "glass ceiling" impeding their opportunities for advancement.

12. _____ are more likely to support Affirmative Action.

13. _____ are more likely to be discriminated against because who they choose to love.

14. _____ are more likely to align themselves with the Republican Party.

15. _____ are more likely to be ignored by the police when driving a very expensive vehicle.

16. _____ are more likely to pray for someone who has treated them poorly.

17. _____ are lazy and would prefer to live off of welfare payments.

18. _____ are more likely to have six or more children.

19. _____ are more likely to enjoy classical music and art museums.

20. _____ are more likely to be members of a country club.

21. _____ are more likely to attend church activities at least three times a week.

22. _____ are more likely to be a CEO of a fortune five hundred business.

23. _____ are more likely to have children who have traveled abroad.

24. _____ are more likely to enroll their children in inner-city public schools.

25. _____ are more likely to be employed to clean the country club.

26. _____ are more likely to wear bright colored clothing and talk very loudly, with profanity, while walking around in the mall.

27. _____ are more likely to come from in a single parent home.

28. _____ are more likely to major in math while in college.

It is suggested here that leaders find ways to diminish the impact of the overly generalized and negative perceptions of difference. It is imperative that leaders find ways to create a culture of inclusion. In this discussion, we are taking about a school culture focused on identifying and utilizing the gifts of all involved. Review the two examples of school culture below and think about how each helps us prepare the next generation for life in a true democracy.

SCHOOL CULTURE – SCENARIO ONE

I believe that the primary goal that schools must embrace is to become a teaching and learning environment dedicated to efforts resulting in learners developing the ability to learn how to learn for themselves. For example, learners will progressively demonstrate the ability to take questions presented to them and conduct research to seek needed answers. Learners will also demonstrate the ability to develop new questions to expand the base of knowledge. Within this teaching and learning environment it is understood that all are both teachers and learners. There exist a high level of excitement about learning, reflecting on knowledge and new questions, and creating new and clearer ways to know.

My role as principal is very important to the successful accomplishment of this goal. I model the results of this goal by visiting classrooms and becoming actively engaged in the teaching and learning that is taking place. I have conversations with teachers, individually and in groups, focused on finding meaning, answers, and new concepts, etc. Similar conversations take place with staff, students, and parents. We have established two "new ideas" resource rooms, one for faculty and staff and the other for students. Learning resources are continually updated in each room. Through self and small group research, we actually create new ways of teaching and learning in these resource rooms. We often discover new ways of thinking and learning about particular topics.

Our campus loves to try new techniques. We celebrate our successes and hold funerals for our failures. In this atmosphere trying new ideas and concepts are encouraged. What a great environment for teaching and learning! I have gained enough cache with district administrators, trustees and community leaders, giving me the ability to interview and select teachers and staff that want to embrace our approach to teaching and learning. State mandated testing takes care of itself resulting in outstanding success. This demonstration of success and the continued student success when they leave us has created a buffer between our school and district mandates. We adhere to all requirements. However, these requirements are taken as baseline activities. We take teaching and learning far beyond what the district curriculum calls for. Our students continue to push the envelop, challenging teachers each day.

Every voice in this teaching and learning environment is important. We all play a significant role in the on-going activities and direction of the school. We have a great school culture.

SCHOOL CULTURE – SCENARIO TWO

The district provides each principal with a set of guidelines to be utilized and strictly followed. These guidelines provide a step by step approach for running the day to day operations of the school. Leading my school in this way brings uniformity to the district. It allows for a very fair and consistent district wide evaluation process. The curriculum provided by district officials, which was purchased from one of the national textbook companies, is designed to prepare students to master the state mandated test. This curriculum also provides lessons that emphasizes the development of proper morals. Citizenships and sportsmanship lessons are also included for most, if not all, grade levels. Students progress from year to year kind of in an assembly line fashion. At each stop, grade level, new information is downloaded into he minds of student.

We model the behaviors that we want students to embrace. I set the agenda of fairness by the way I interact with teachers. Making full use of the district's guidelines in chapter eleven. Chapter four in the book of guidelines for teachers provides a step by step blueprint for interacting with students in the classroom. Similar chapters address parent, staff, and community stakeholder interaction. District guideline provide clear and consistent procedures for running every facet of schooling.

I am especially proud of how well these sets of procedures work. We have very few discipline issues with our students. When we do, our zero tolerance for just about every negative behavior results in students transferring to our alternative school site for a minimum of one semester. Faculty and staff know evaluation procedures because every step is scripted and must be followed.

District policies and guidelines provide an excellent blueprint leading to the kind of school culture that, in our opinion, maximizes each student's level of success on state mandated test. Guidelines also tell us how to behave. This makes my job much easier. I simply refer to the guidelines and follow the steps provided to address any issues that might emerge. Each set of guidelines, for me, teachers, students, and parents, provides step by step directions to address just about every imaginable situation. We have a great school culture.

When comparing these two scenarios, which leader is positioned better, philosophically, to create and sustain the kind of teaching and learning environment of inclusion that will prepare learners for life in a true democracy? I think that you can successfully answer this question. Engaged leaders welcome discussions, debates, varying viewpoints. They understand and value different perspectives. Engaged leaders believe that more informed decisions emerge from the kind of environment that promotes the inclusion of all voices.

Therefore, it is suggested here that a process of on-going conscious reflection is needed for those who aspire to become effective engaged leaders. Reflections should compare thoughts, actions and outcomes, especially as they relate to one's ability to lead effectively. One question that deserves reflection from those considered to be effective engaged leaders is: How does my personal culture impact my actions as a leader?

How can a leader effectively explore the filters (culture) through which she/he views and lives her/his life? These filters (education, parents/family, media, religion, friends, etc.) influence who we are, how we think, what we believe to be right and good, and how we act out on these sets of premises; filters; our own personal culture. Giroux (1997) suggest, "how we understand and come to know ourselves cannot be separated from how we are represented and how we imagine ourselves" (p. 15).

You will note that I talk about culture as an individual phenomenon. Most literature describes culture from a group perspective. These descriptions have as a basic premise that culture consist of behaviors, beliefs, morals, art, customs and other characteristics that determine a person's status in a society. However, since culture represents those perspectives within one's life experiences; and since each individual's experiences are unique; it is suggested here that the individual interpretations of experiences and how they impact one's beliefs and actions makes culture not a group but rather an individual phenomenon. Groups of people may have similar foundational ideologies from which culture emerges. However personal experiences often impact individuals in unique ways, resulting in a culture of one.

Embracing this concept of culture clears the pathway for engaged leaders who value the gifts of each member of the organization. This concept of culture moves leaders away from generalizes beliefs about people to more of an individualized approach. The approach results less in enabling groups within the organizations and more towards empowering individuals in ways that increase positive outcomes, both for the organization and the individual.

One way to address this question in a way that brings clarity to answers is by analyzing one's philosophy of leadership as it relates to the culture of the organization. The following questionnaire can be used to help leaders see where they are from this perspective.

What is Your Philosophy of Leadership: as it Relates to the Culture of the Organization?

Please check the answer under each item that best reflects your current thinking.

1. What should be the atmosphere within a diverse community?
    A. All people, regardless of their identity, striving to work and live together.
    B. All striving to learn more about and gain a greater respect for the groups within our community.
    C. All striving to embrace traditional values that lead all to common goals.
    D. All striving to learn from each other and using this knowledge to help our community.

2. What should be the role of primary leadership in working within a diverse community?
    A. Consistent with our demographics, leadership should develop an appreciation for differences.
    B. Leadership should, based on traditional standardized measures, promote common values and goals.
    C. Leadership should actively work with the various groups that make up the community.
    D. Leadership should wisely use the strengths of the individuals that make up the community.

3. What foundational premise best guides your thoughts about our changing demographics?
    A. We should do all we can to assimilate every citizen.
    B. We should find ways for each identity group to express a presence in the society.
    C. We should become familiar with each group and their cultural perspectives.
    D. We should include all individuals as members of and positive contributors to the society.

4. What is the role of education in a diverse community?
    A. Learn truth, which is absolute, universal, and unchanging.
    B. Learn about other identity groups within the content of course work.
    C. Learn to accept other ways of thinking and living.
    D. Empower each individual to learn how to learn for themselves.

5. How should we make our environment accessible for the physically challenged?
    A. Based on available funds and within the overall budgetary priorities of the campus community.
    B. Develop special programs to meet the needs of and create a better awareness about the physically challenged
    C. Meeting federal standards in the most cost-effective way.
    D. Utilize the gifts and abilities of the physically challenged as a way to define and envision community.

6. What foundational premise best guides your thoughts about religion?
    A. We are a nation built on Christian values. These are our guiding principles.
    B. We should not condemn those who are not Christians.
    C. We should actively utilize the values and insights from the many different religions to enhance clarity and understanding.
    D. We should acknowledge and respect many religions.

7. What foundational premise best guides your thoughts about race?
    A. Race is a socially constructed phenomenon that is embraced by individuals in various ways.
    B. People represent different groups that should be understood.
    C. Race is biologically based, making certain attributes superior to others.
    D. Acceptance for each race is important in building a diverse society.

8. What foundational premise best guides your thoughts about sexual orientations?
    A. Homosexuals are sinners
    B. We should inform learners about sexual orientations.
    C. The complexities of sexual orientations are expressed in different ways, from individual to individual.
    D. We should acknowledge biological and other components in identity and personal choice.

9. What foundational premise best guides your thoughts about the poor?
    A. It is the natural way of things.
    B. Represents a group of people in most societies.
    C. One of numerous characteristics that a person might include as part of their identity at some point in time.
    D. The poor are people too.

10 What foundational premise best guides your thoughts about the contributions of each gender?
    A. Men are the breadwinners of the family.
    B. Men and women have unique gifts that should be wisely used for success.
    C. We should allow women opportunities to lead.
    D. Men and women have unique gifts that we should understand and respect.

(Adapted from Glickman: What Is Your Philosophy of Supervision)

The following four descriptions are used to score the questionnaire. It helps us better understand why we think and act in certain ways.

Assimilation/Essentialism Perspective

The practice of categorizing a group based on an artificial social construction that imparts an "essence" of that group, which homogenizes the group and effaced individuality and differences. This perspective implies that we are forming conclusions, relationships, and other cultural ties based only on the essential elements as determined by "us". It also implies that there are some minimal levels of understanding that is applied to groups.

The concept as described here assumes that there is one best way to do and/or think about something. In some instances one could find support for this assumption. For example, most, if not all, of us would agree that there would be fewer accidents if all drivers followed the rules of the road. Our cities would be safer is we all agreed that hurting others is something we never do.

- Certain words and phrases come to mind when thinking about this description. Standardize – to make, cause, or adopt to fit a certain standard.
- Traditional Values – time honored practices, a set of highly valued customs passed on from one generation to the next.
- Conservative – the preservation of the existing order, to resist or oppose change or innovation.
- Myopic – shortsightedness, lack of discernment in thinking or looking towards the future.
- Myths – the belief that groups of people are all the same.

TOLERANCE PERSPECTIVE

There is an acceptance and open-mindedness of different practices, attitudes, and cultures but does not necessarily mean agreement with the differences. The word implies an acknowledgement, or an acceptance. However the word does not necessarily acknowledge an appreciate of differences and usually consists of only surface level information and commitment. The concept of tolerance described here expresses an acceptance of differences, but not a deep understanding or valuing of them.

Certain words and phrases come to mind when thinking about is description.

- Impersonal – to be distant, disconnected, remote, uncommitted.
- Political Correctness – to be polite, courteous, civil, deferential, well-mannered.

MULTICULTURAL PERSPECTIVE

The practice of acknowledging and respecting the various cultures, religions, races, ethnicities, attitudes and opinions within an environment. The word does not imply that there is any intentionality occurring and primarily works from a group, versus individual, orientation. The concept of multiculturalism described here focuses on group representation. It fails to see the individual. It also does little to move from a generalized understanding of differences to actions that embrace and include others as individuals.

Certain words and phrases come to mind when thinking about this description.

- Group Representation – people are understood using group identifiers. It is a form of dehumanization because the individual is ignored, invisible.
- Enable – to permit, help but not allow to become self-empowered.
- Stereotype – to reinforce existing generalizations about groups of people.
- Respect – to relate and/or acknowledge concern for groups (not individuals) of people.

INCLUSION PERSPECTIVE

The practice of emphasizing our uniqueness in promoting the realty that each voice, when valued, respected and expected to, will provide positive contributions to the community. We become actively engaged in getting to know the person.

Certain words come to mind when thinking about this description.

Empower – we value the individual and work to diminish perceptual and real barriers that impede full community membership.

- Voice – all voices in the community bring synergy to discussions which lead to better informed decisions.
- Individual – we see each person as a unique person, full of positive potential and worthy of equal membership.

Let's take a look at question number one: What should be the atmosphere within a diverse community?

- All people striving to embrace traditional values that lead all to share common goals = Assimilation.
- All people, regardless of their identity, striving to work and live together = Tolerance.
- All people striving to learn more about and gain a greater respect for the groups within our community = Multiculturalism.
- All people striving to learn from each other and using this knowledge to help our community achieve collaboratively developed goals = Inclusiviness.

One of the first steps towards effective change is the realization of the need for it. The answers to this questionnaire will assist individuals who want to see a need for change. The chart below provides the answers to the questionnaire.

Please check the answer under each item that best reflects your current thinking.

1. What should be the atmosphere within a diverse community?
    A. All people, regardless of their identity, striving to work and live together.
    B. All striving to learn more about and gain a greater respect for the groups within our community.
    C. All striving to embrace traditional values that lead all to common goals.
    D. All striving to learn from each other and using this knowledge to help our community.

2. What should be the role of primary leadership in working within a diverse community?
    A. Consistent with our demographics, leadership should develop an appreciation for differences.
    B. Leadership should, based on traditional standardized measures, promote common values and goals.
    C. Leadership should actively work with the various groups that make up the community.
    D. Leadership should wisely use the strengths of the individuals that make up the community.

3. What foundational premise best guides your thoughts about our changing demographics?
    A. We should do all we can to assimilate every citizen.
    B. We should find ways for each identity group to express a presence in the society.
    C. We should become familiar with each group and their cultural perspectives.
    D. We should include all individuals as members of and positive contributors to the society.

4. What is the role of education in a diverse community?
    A. Learn truth, which is absolute, universal, and unchanging.
    B. Learn about other identity groups within the content of course work.
    C. Learn to accept other ways of thinking and living.
    D. Empower each individual to learn how to learn for themselves.

5. How should we make our environment accessible for the physically challenged?
    A. Based on available funds and within the overall budgetary priorities of the campus community.
    B. Develop special programs to meet the needs of and create a better awareness about the physically challenged?
    C. Meeting federal standards in the most cost-effective way.
    D. Utilize the gifts and abilities of the physically challenged as a way to define and envision community.

6. What foundational premise best guides your thoughts about religion?
    A. We are a nation built on Christian values. These are our guiding principles.
    B. We should not condemn those who are not Christians.
    C. We should actively utilize the values and insights from the many different religions to enhance clarity and understanding.
    D. We should acknowledge and respect many religions.

7. What foundational premise best guides your thoughts about race?
    A. A Race is a socially constructed phenomenon that is embraced by individuals in various ways.
    B. People represent different groups that should be understood.
    C. Race is biologically based, making certain attributes superior to others.
    D. Acceptance for each race is important in building a diverse society.

8. What foundational premise best guides your thoughts about sexual orientation?
    A. Homosexuals are sinners
    B. We should inform learners about sexual orientations.
    C. The complexities of sexual orientations are expressed in different ways, from individual to individual.
    D. We should acknowledge biological and other components in identity and personal choice.

9. What foundational premise best guides your thoughts about the poor?
    A. It is the natural way of things.
    B. Represents a group of people in most societies.
    C. One of numerous characteristics that a person might include as part of their identity at some point in time.
    D. The poor are people too.

10. What foundational premise best guides your thoughts about the contributions of each gender?
    A. Men are the breadwinners of the family.
    B. Men and women have unique gifts that should be wisely used for success.
    C. We should allow women opportunities to lead.
    D. Men and women have unique gifts that we should understand and respect.

Assimilation   Tolerance   Multiculturalism   Inclusion

Translations

Members of a learning community that expects everyone to think and act alike are practicing Assimilation.

Members of a learning community that merely accommodates one or two individuals who are different from the rest of the group, but never allows full membership, as they are, are practicing Tolerance.

Members of a learning community that interacts with "others" based on some set of predetermined generalized group characteristics are practicing Multiculturalism.

Members of a learning community that are actively broadening their perspectives about differences, actively seeking to get to know individuals, and actively including all members of the community are practicing Inclusion.

How did we forget that our differences are among our most valuable assets? What happened to "we have nothing to fear but fear itself?" When will we learn that violence in the long run creates at least as many problems as it solves? Why do we not value life, every life, no matter whose or where? Or understand that the measure of national greatness is not only how successful the strong can be but how well we support the weak? (Palmer, 2011, pg. 2).

Leaders in today's school environments, and other organizations, must continue to listen, learn and better utilize the knowledge and skills of other stakeholders. These leaders must be able to function in an ever evolving teaching and learning environment. Similar to the ethos of engaged pedagogy, engaged leadership assumes that every stakeholder has valuable contributions to make that will improve the organization. The engaged leader inspires participation, encourages meaningful working relationships between stakeholders, and is enthusiastic about the possibilities that emerge from this type of dynamic, interactive, inclusive process. The proposition here is that leadership must be inclusive of the voices of all stakeholders.

But democracy itself is still a means. And it is a means for the flowering of individuality. Why do I see it this way? Because I stand fundamentally on the profoundly Christian notion that we are each made equal in the eyes of God. That Rockefeller has the same status as a peasant in Alabama. And that peasant in Alabama has the same right to human flourishing as any other human being regardles of race, regardless of religion, regardless of nation, regardless of gender. It is a deep, spiritually based notion of equality. Doesn't mean that we have the same natural capacities. Doesn't mean that we have the same natural talents. But we ought to have the same opportunities. We ought to have the same chances (West, 1993, 0.63).

It is suggested here that in order to be an engaged leader, one must also practice democracy (inclusion). It is further suggested here that organizations increase productivity when inclusion best describes the work environment.

REFERENCES

Ellsworth, E. (1989). Why Doesn't This Feel Empowering?: Working Through the Repressive Myths of Critical Pedagogy. Harvard Educational Review 59, no. 3: 297–324.

Freire, P. (1998). Pedagogy of the Oppressed. New York: Continuum.

Giroux, H. (1997). Channel Surfing: Race Talk and the Destruction of Today's Youth. New York: St. Martin's Press.

Hooks, B. (1994). Teaching to Transgress: Education as the Practice of Freedom. New York: Routledge.

Koppelman, K. (2011). Understanding Human Differences: Multicultural Education for a Diverse America. Boston, MA: Allyn & Bacon.

Larson, C. and Murtadha, K. (2003). Leadership for Social Justice. In J. Murphy (Ed.), The Educational Leadership Challenge: Redefining Leadership for the 21st Century (pp. 134–161). Chicago: University of Chicago Press.

Nieto, S. (2008). Affirming Diversity: The Sociopolitical Context of Multicultural Education: Boston, MA. Allyn & Bacon.

Palmer, P. (2011). Healing the Heart of Democracy. San Francisco, CA. Jossey-Bass.

Shields, C. (2004). Dialogic Leadership for Social Justice: Overcoming Pathologies of Silence. Educational Administration Quarterly Vol. 40, No. 1 pp. 109–132.

Steele, C.M. (1997). A Threat in the Air: How Stereotypes Shape Intellectual Identity and Performance. American Psychologist 52, pp. 613–629.

Thomas, C. (2003). Transgressing Culture Lines. Dubuque, Iowa: Kendall Hunt Publishers.

Tyack, D. and Hansot, E. (1982). Managers of Virtue. New York: Basic Books.

West, C. (1993). Race Matters. Boston: Beacon Press.

CHAPTER 7

ACTIONS OF AN ENGAGED LEADER

There are people in America who overemphasize our unity yet fail to appreciate the importance of our diversity, just as there are those who emphasize our diversity yet fail to appreciate the importance of our unity. It is to appreciate the importance of our unity. It is imperative that we honor both. It is our unity and our diversity that matters, and their relationship to each other reflects a philosophical and political truth outside of which we cannot thrive.

Williamson, 1997, pg. 72

INTRODUCTION

I became the Special Assistant to the Chancellor for Diversity and Community at Texas Christian University in, I believe January, 2000. Before this change I served as an Associate Professor and Department Chair for Educational Foundations and Administration in the then School of Education. One of the first actions taken in this office focused on bringing clarity to the work ahead. These actions led to the development of a pamphlet describing our work. John Butler, then University Minister, (my partner in crime), and I wrote this document. I share parts of this document below. I will attempt to connect these thoughts with the work of engaged leaders later in this chapter.

DIVERSITY – INCLUSION – ENGAGED LEADERSHIP

Today, the word 'diversity' often appears in the variety of places we experience community (work settings, schools, churches, etc.). Immediately, there are images that come to mind, some comfortable, some threatening, some helpful to self and others. The word carries with it many complex reactions and many complex dimensions. Approaching that complexity will require a rich variety of experiences, steps and stages, policies and procedures that involve every place we are organized for life together and involve all the people who share those places.

People everywhere are living with every aspect of their lives connected to a global society. Almost every culture can be found almost everywhere. Wherever we are busy with life we will find the world in people with whom we will be engaged. Our environment, health, clothing, transportation, technology, medicines, education, and most everything that shapes the quality of life occurs on a global scale. In many ways we are at a critical point of change in the history of the world. Those persons who are comfortable, respectful, informed about, and engaged with life in that global society will be successful (socially, emotionally, even economically); those who are not able to achieve this level of comfort and capacity will find themselves in increasing trouble in the coming years. A global society is not some fad or a political notion that will go away. Already, the change that has occurred would require the demise of our culture to re-establish some notion of "what is was like in the good old days." These factors have led people across the society to draw upon one another to make the most of the changing realities to achieve the best living-working situation for all people involved.

Often there are reactions to the word diversity and they include avoidance at one end and a sense of completion on the other. Avoidance frequently carries with it feelings of anger, claims of some established and somehow reliable solidarity, some degree of defensiveness, and a denial that there is anything to explore. It is perceived that "*there are not problems and if there are, that is the way it is supposed to be.*" Others will have the perception that diversity is not something to be avoided, that it is real and important, "*I just happen to have already completed the work that is needed.*" This feeling carries with it a level of comfort in certain assumptions, a clarity that others have work to do, that prejudices and injustices reside everywhere. "*I don't have any prejudices, I treat everyone the same. I know what we need to talk about, and if there are problems, others will need to explore their problem. I don't have a problem with anyone.*" Given the history of our country and how diversity work has begun in recent times, both reactions are natural and to be expected. It is appropriate to accept both reactions as part of the landscape of relationships. If those who have either response will journey even for a short time into the work of diversity and inclusiveness they will discover that their reaction is only that, a reaction. Both will turn out to be unsupported by rational understanding and not helpful to self or the community as we work toward a better future for all of us.

Diversity work is not an experience, or scheduled event, or a workshop or a set of skills, rather, it is a process of becoming that begins wherever we are individually and collectively with our comforts and capacities, leading into the future. Diversity work is like working with a fabric or a mosaic working toward completion, using who we are in an active interaction and active commitment to end insensitivity, intolerance, and prejudices that weaken the society we are becoming. And while work on the connections certainly occurs in a workshop or in a personal encounter, new people will come into the environment, new insights will occur, and new dynamics from beyond us will each require us to change. The combination of personal commitments, policies, and laws guide the process, but do not guarantee or adequately respond to the process of change that is occurring in the world. Diversity work is thus a never-ending process. For the foreseeable future, as the world makes its change and we are part of that change, all of us will be engaged in diversity work, (positive and/or negative) in a rich variety of settings.

When we say the word diversity, many of us think, "Oh, I know what that is about, we are going to talk about those others." There is, of course, much to learn and thoroughly incorporate about others around us. The world is large and complex when it comes to cultural identities. The experiences of those around the country already doing diversity work, the overwhelming time and energy will be spent learning about self as we each become individually part of the new reality around us. There is much to learn about self in diversity work and the result not only will help us in the changes, but will help others in their changes. Self and others are two sides of the same essential experience of learning in this work. There are several other combinations that will guide and enrich the work ahead.

The rich diversity within each of us (how do I understand love, achievement, honesty, compassion, and many other elements in identity) impacts the quality and extent of our diversity work. They are each a complex and unfolding mix of realities within us; each contributing to the other in significant ways. This is the diversity within us. And yet there is that reality out beyond us, which behaves in more complex, but similar ways; the Internal and External sides of diversity. We each grew up with an understanding of whether or not we are part of the majority or the minority (for example, racially, politically, religiously speaking). And yet, based upon the setting and changing circumstances we will find ourselves moving from one to the other and back again. All of us understand there are differences between us and we want to respect and affirm those differences. And yet if all we worked on in diversity work and in social settings were the differences, very soon there would be significant pressure to affirm a particular, what would be seen as pure form of a given difference. And that purity would be sought to be the absolute expression of a difference, destroying society in the declaration of it. We have seen those declarations in history and contemporarily. Another side is needed. The work for the common good becomes essential. We appreciate the differences, but see that we have common hopes and needs, and that common connection is good for all. And yet, if all that was sought was the common good, very soon there would be efforts to have common language, common dress, and common values. The result may make some people feel better, but the result destroys personhood. Both work for differences and the common good are essential. And that is the case for all of the two-sided coins of diversity. And there were more than were mentioned here; Here and Everywhere; Now and a Very Long Time; One Culture and All Cultures. Each of these are coins for investing time, energy, hopes, comforts, and capacities for the sake of the future. We will be back and forth between each side of each coin as circumstances demand. Leaders and those successful in the changes occurring in the world will move smoothly and easily between both sides. Those fisted on one side of a particular coin will be a problem for themselves and the community. All of these coins and others will be required to make the investment in diversity work for the future that is unfolding.

A PROCESS OF BECOMING

When considering our thoughts expressed here regarding diversity, what kinds of teaching and learning environments will effectively serve the students at your university or school? What role does the teaching/learning process play in this learning environment? What are the roles of the individuals who are members of this community of leaners? To answer these questions we must first have a vision depicting the type of individuals we want our students to become and the society in which they will live. We would suggest that we want to help develop individuals oriented towards a life of active, self-directed learning, critical inquiry, reflective thinking and prepared to serve by searching for what we can become instead of just being satisfied with the way things currently are. If this premise has any merit we must then choose the types of learning environments and experiences that will help us achieve these goals. Should we also, as part of our responsibility in this teaching and learning process, facilitate the continuous process of learning education leaders must experience in order to remain effective?

What responses most accurately answer these thoughts? Do we listen to popular constructivist discussions about preferred learning environments and believe we are moving towards doing the right thing? Will looking at campus/school environments, our evolving global community and current student beliefs and actions bring validity to these discussions or reinforce the need to continue without much change? In other words, how do we view the global community and our role in preparing students for this new world?

How we think and what we believe help to form the foundation from which we live our lives and interact with others. These two factors can either enhance or hinder how we provide growth opportunities for individuals. Similar to building bridges, if foundational components are not internalized then attempts to build on such foundations have little chance of successfully sustaining challenges that are sure to occur during one's life. The building process is doomed from the very beginning. Our approach consists of three stages.

MOVING THROUGH STAGES

Everyone approaches the work of diversity, whether on campus or in corporations in the larger society, through stages. No one experiences inclusiveness in a single conversion experience, or educational encounter, or a workshop of days or a week. It happens in stages and in fact, one might more accurately say, we, as individuals and as organizations, rotate through stages, beginning, completing, and beginning again. Life circumstances and our own capacities both move us through the stages and force us to make the journey again. It might easily be said to those who say, "*well, I know all there is to know of diversity. I have done all that,*" it is good you have done what you have, but most of us have hardly even begun. The immediate community and the global community are rapidly changing in demographics and in issues that give our community its reality. No one is ever finished in this continuously unfolding and expanding process. It is a journey toward an inclusiveness that has no precise end because people and issues and new understandings of the two sided coins are reappearing new, unexpected, and transforming ways.

Different authors propose a variety of stages ranging from four to six identifiable, testable, and reliable stages. While these are important to know and appreciated, we are proposing that they can be reduced to a simple set of three stages.

IDENTITY

The first stage is a set of experiences, encounters, integrations, and self-understandings that lead to identity formation and a declaration for all to know. This is who I am and how I am able to declare; here I stand. Coming to this certainly includes a personal sense of well-being, health, cultural histories, traditions, symbols, personal experiences, and all that defines a person and how that person is part of a larger culture. Identify is of course more than our own expression of who we are. There are so many cultures and so many people within each. Some people have not thought of their identity within the interplay of others, while some have well begun the process. Caucuses and other group experiences that help present the identity and the rich variety of ways of gathering people within an identity are all part of this stage. Thinking, engaging, withdrawing, reflecting, coming back to engage again, asserting, reshaping, and integrating are each pieces of this important stage. More to the point of being in the work of diversity, this stage includes finding the space to do this work not only for one's own cultural identity, but to allow and encourage others to be about the same process. This stage is almost continuously reoccurring as new people become part of the community, bringing new ways and new opportunities for being a particular identity. This stage is not merely the first stage; it is the foundational encounter with self and with others in which all dimensions and elements in the diversity work impact the self, with self-impacting others. To say that this stage is exciting and creative is an understatement. The power it brings to individuals, groups of individuals, and to the community that knows it emerges out of the capacities of everyone to declare a strong, vibrant, and contributing identity.

PRESENCE

Once a person and/or groups understand who it is (rather who it is becoming), there is the need both for that group and for the larger community to experiences the presence of that group. What is it that the group or culture has to say to all of us? What is it that they have to say to particular individuals within the larger organization or community? How will they say it? How will they impact the on-going life of the community? These questions and others point to a process of recognition, respect and appreciation, honoring, and enabling the presence (physically, organizationally, and interpersonally) in all dimensions of the organization or community. This stage is both the standing to declare a difference made because of the particular identity, but it is also the act of making room for, giving credence and appreciation for the presence of the identities that form the community. This will be a dynamic, potentially loud, and always changing stage for everyone in the organization. To truly encounter the presence of a population is to address many of the coins described earlier that are the investment in the success of self and the success of the particular community. This stage will be a most rewarding and highly visible stage, but the one stage among the three where tension emerges, issues are defined in new ways and the content of the future comes into clearer and clearer focus. Because of you and you and you and me, we will be different.

INTENTIONALITY

What we do with who we are together becomes the essential test of both of the earlier stages. Whether we can make our community stronger, more successful, more effective in who we really are for ourselves is as vital an issue for the organization as it is for a single individual. This is the moral, character defining, value laden, social-economic, political moment of making a difference in the larger global community. It has to make a difference that we have come to a full awareness of who we are and what we have to do as a result of that as an outcome. Will there be fairness and justice in our relationships and in the world? What difference does it make that we exist together? Will we be able to create a new community that better understands who we are and that is better prepared to receive the on-coming realities of the world yet to be? This is the process of accountability with one another and with the future generation. This is the stage in which we apply the other two stages for an outcome that is marked by the best in who we are and the hope in the best in who we must yet be for the future. This is the stage where alliances and commitments to be a community take shape. This stage is marked by moral and political choices, by discoveries of our similarities in purpose, by our commitment to inclusiveness for everyone, including those who have not yet appeared or emerged. It is a raucous and yet rewarding stage that turns the immediate community into just that, a community, and establishes the hope for the global community that is still taking form.

As we repeatedly move through each stage, due to changes in self and others, we become more capable of establishing the inclusiveness that comes only through all voices. Inclusiveness is a measurable, desirable, changeable and renewable outcome. The community will in the long run have reached its most effective goal because of who formed it and how they are able to work together. There are other approaches to organizational and community life: dictatorships, effectiveness training, quality assurance, and others. But none will have voices of all participants and move to include the full connections to the global community as the process of inclusiveness.

We must create opportunities for individuals to become more understanding, thoughtful, and expressive about issues that impact their lives. All must have opportunities to "Voice" their opinions in the community. With these thoughts and stages as our foundation, we suggest *Inclusiveness* as a possible approach to achieve desired goals.

INCLUSIVENESS

The concept of inclusiveness has often been used to force homogenization or to create the image that we are a "melting pot" of identities, creating a single notion of culture and community. We believe, however, in the concept of inclusiveness that leads to a synthesis of thoroughly understood and strongly declared identities which lead to actions that shape the good of a realistically diverse community. Inclusiveness, we believe, builds a stronger campus community, city, nation and world in three powerful and interrelated ways. First, by emphasizing our uniqueness in promoting the reality that each voice makes when valued, respected and expected to provide positive contributions to the community. Emphasizing our uniqueness will bring support as all members of a community work toward making the traditional hierarchical structures of identity flatten into a continuum of descriptions and beliefs that bring value, energy, and synergy to an organization. In other words, we begin to understand that difference does not automatically mean *less than*, but rather different. These declarations of "*Identity*" provide an invaluable gift to persons and to the process toward inclusiveness. Second that a commitment to the worth and dignity of people expressed in their uniqueness brings synergy to a community. Our willingness to both declare "*Presence*" and an openness to receive presence across a variety of identities provides an atmosphere where collaboration empowers the complexity of our life with others. Broadening our perspectives and capacity to relate to people and ideas will help us better understand the societal dynamics, which need improving. Third, understanding the dynamics in our society which need improving from this perspective will help people recognize that we are all part of the synergy and systems where heritage is a resource and not a barrier, where hopes are shaped by our interdependence and not upon imposed separation. Broadening our perspectives about issues and experiences can create "*Intentionality*" – new pathways of understanding, more productive and real relationships, and empower others to become active contributors towards the betterment of the community. Much of this work is addressed as we seek answers to the following questions:

- What expressions of identity are forming in the community?
- What causes and events and organizations are allowing for identity here?
- How can we create an atmosphere where presence is anticipated and desired?
- Is there a particular presence burgeoning that we need to hear and incorporate?
- What are the organizational opportunities to form an intentionality that will change our community toward inclusiveness?
- What connections are happening between persons and cultures that can change our community?
- Can we recognize where people are in their journey toward inclusiveness?
- Can we recognize where our community is in its journey toward inclusiveness?

Answers to these and similar questions bring focus to the issue at hand, what can we do to create a more inclusive community of learners on our college/school campuses?

STEPPING TOWARDS INCLUSIVENESS

We developed a questionnaire entitled "What Is Your Philosophy of Diversity?" that has proven to open the doors of conversation about the issues that impact our relationships with others. This questionnaire, and the discussions that follow, help participants begin to see what they really believe about certain issues, of even greater importance, why. This is how the process typically works. Participants are asked to complete the short questionnaire. They are told that we will not collect the questionnaire, so please answer each question as honestly as possible. We tell them we will ask later for volunteers to share their thoughts, and possibly their responses, regarding the questionnaire. Each participant is given a scoring chart along with our definitions for each of the four descriptors. Before asking for volunteers to share their thoughts, we review the definitions and ask participants to look at the results of their answers along a continuum of thought versus looking at them from a traditional hierarchical perspective. We say that given particular situations and our personal record of experiences that greatly influence our beliefs, we are at various stages of thought. For example, one of us might say; "*In certain situations, the concept of assimilation can be good. We all assimilate in some ways. For example, I believe we should all abide by traffic speed limits; I think that certain rules regarding my job, like wearing clothes, must be honored; I think we should not liter, etc. My point is we cannot have any degree of freedom without some rules. We must all adhere to levels of uniformity at certain points in our lives.*" Or one of us might say: "*While I support the importance of understanding cultural aspects, I must do more. I need to get to know the individual in order to develop the kind of working relationship needed to be as successful as possible in this venture. I am also excited about learning, broadening my perspectives beyond the generalization talked about. There is so much more to an individual than some set of descriptors.*"

An activity entitled "Key Words" brings more understanding to these issues (see Appendix A). We will share three key words that come to mind when thinking about the four categories (descriptors) from the questionnaire (see chapter six). We then break the participants into four small groups and ask them to share three additional words from one of the eleven categories along with why these words where chosen. People become more engaged in the process. They begin to connect our work with their personal life experiences. Participants begin to express the need for change within themselves, their families, work environments and our society.

We typically are forced to shorten discussions at this time for the sake of limited time. Our next activity is designed to help participants internalize these issues even more. We present a new set of questions to participants based on the group we are working with (see appendix B). In small groups, participants are asked to develop statements that would demonstrate a point of view for each of the four descriptors in use. For example, we might present the following question:

How should we deal with conflict centered on issues of social economic status between students?

Each group will be asked to develop a statement, similar to ones shared on the questionnaire, which would answer this question for each of the four descriptors. The expansion of issues has no limits as participants begin to develop their own series of additional questions. We begin to see more clearly that **how we think and what we believe help to direct our actions**. This process will also help us become more reflective before making decisions. Often we are challenged, internally, to change the way we think and what we believe – and to change our actions.

There is indeed much work to be done. This work is never complete. What I share here is a starting point worthy of serious consideration. I understand that this process is only one of many choices one can make. The importance of a process that looks more at self than the other should not be ignored. It should not be considered too *touchy-feely*. Rather, it is intense and valuable work. As previously stated, diversity work . . . "is a process of becoming that begins wherever we are individually and collectively with our comfort and capacities, leading into the future." It is strongly suggested here that this model enhances these efforts.

CONNECTIONS

The most exciting aspect of critical thinking in the classroom is that it calls for initiative from everyone, actively inviting all students to think passionately and to share ideas in a passionate, open manner. When everyone in the classroom, teacher and students, recognizes that they are responsible for creating a learning community together, learning is at its most meaningful and useful. In such a community of learning there is no failure. Everyone is participating and sharing whatever resource is needed at a given moment in time to ensure that we leave the classroom knowing that critical thinking empowers us.

Hooks, 2010, pg. 10.

How do these thoughts about inclusion impact the actions of the engaged leader in public school settings? Of course staff development and other professional growth activities designed to enhance personal and organizational growth in this area is essential. However, to further address this question, I will briefly connect the stages of identity, presence, and intentionality to the role of engaged leadership. I will then review three questions asked earlier in this chapter:

- What kinds of teaching and learning environments will effectively serve the students in your school?
- What role does the teaching and learning process play in this learning environment?
- What are the roles of the individuals who are members of this community of leaders?

IDENTITY

As previously expressed, identity relates to, "who I am and how I am able to declare here I stand." This call for identity becomes important because it causes individuals to recognize their strengths and weakness; their place in the world; and the gifts that they individually possess to help make the world a better place for all. The engaged leader values this notion of identity. He/she understands the value each person's gifts to an organization. Therefore the engaged leader works to build the kind of environment that promotes identity of self, of others, and of the community. He/she utilizes the building of one to one relationships, linked with a pathway of connections. These pathways of connections are utilized by teachers to help learners connect prior knowledge with new information in ways that help to internalize meaning and to create new meaning. This pathway of connections is paved with the kinds of relationships between teachers and learners that become a conduit for a growing web of understanding of who I am; who you are; how we each learn; and how best to share new information that is internalized. Of course we all realize that the role of teacher and learner changes from time to time. In these settings, administrators, teachers, staff, students, parents, and other stakeholders are all teachers and learners at given points of the life of the school.

The engaged leader models these behaviors in their work with all teachers and learners that are a part of the organization. They strive to better understand each individual, their strengths and weaknesses; likes and dislikes; prior knowledge; best learning styles, etc. Engaged leaders then use this knowledge to bridge gaps of understanding, making links that did not exist and thus finding ways for all to voice their thoughts in ways that inform and improve the work to be done.

PRESENCE

This process of inclusion that is utilized by engaged leaders creates an atmosphere of sharing. Individulas are excited about being a part of a community of learners where recognition of self, respect and appreciation of self and the empowering of self are points of focus. The engaged leader strives to understand the needs of each individual. These actions, in turn, cause others to actively understand themselves and others. A better and more valued understanding of 'I' results in a better and more valued understanding of "we".

INTENTIONALITY

The 'we' described above enhances our efforts towards fairness; justice for all; a community striving to accomplish and exceed stated goals. The engaged leader strives to build such a community of teachers and learners. The engaged leader works hard to build a community of 'we' where accountability, dependability, and excellence thrives.

Some would argue that this atmosphere of inclusion in our public schools can only be imagined. It can never really exist. They would further argue that the need for most, if not all, of us to develop a sense of self, identify, on the backs of others will not allow for any significant community of inclusion. In other words, some would argue that human nature causes individuals to seek power. This premise is supported by the belief that those in power define themselves in ways that justify their position in society. They glorify themselves, while vilifying others. History, they would tell us, provides all of the needed support for their argument. I would help them to remember that this system of identity has also cloaked the dangers ahead and have led to the destruction of each of these societies. The illumination of these examples in history, one would hope, should cause all of us to take a different path. I simply provide a counter argument by asking if we are truly satisfied with the current culture within our public schools. Of greater concern, are we satisfied to travel along similar pathways that have historically had disastrous results?

Therefore, the engaged leaders establishes a teaching and learning environment built on trust. By trust I mean that teachers and learners will do all that they can to ensure that learning does occur at the highest possible levels. The atmosphere is one of inquiry, risk-taking, and self-directed learning. There exist a community that values the discussion of varying viewpoints, critical and reflective thinking; and demonstrated joy for learning.

Both teachers and learners support one another. They see learners, not as receptacles to simply pour knowledge in, but rather souls full of knowledge seeking to realize, to know even more.

Leadership then facilitates in ways that clears this pathway of interactive, engaged, and often self-directed teaching and learning of the barriers that might impede travel. They support, provide funding, and direction when needed. Engaged leaders do all that they possibly can to make sure this type of teaching and learning environment continues to evolve.

Then imagine with me the possibilities of the future of public schooling. Let us walk together as we step into this era of engaged leadership and inclusion in our public schools.

REFERENCES

Hooks, B. (2010). Teaching Critical Thinking: Practical Wisdom. New York: Routledge.
Williamson, Marianne. (1997). The Healing of America. New York: Simon and Schuster.

KEY WORDS

Essentialism/ Assimilation	Tolerance	Multicultural	Inclusiveness
Traditional Values	Impersonal	Group Representation	Group Representation
Control	Accommodate	Enable	Empower
Standard	Political Correctness	Respect	Voice
_____	_____	_____	_____
_____	_____	_____	_____
_____	_____	_____	_____
_____	_____	_____	_____
_____	_____	_____	_____
_____	_____	_____	_____
_____	_____	_____	_____
_____	_____	_____	_____
_____	_____	_____	_____
_____	_____	_____	_____

DEVELOPING NEW QUESTIONS

What foundational premise best guides our thoughts about learning?
E.
T.
M.
I.

What foundational premise best guides our thoughts about leadership?
E.
T.
M.
I.

How should the thoughts of other stakeholders be best handled?
E.
T.
M.
I.

CHAPTER 8

THE POWER OF CONVERSATIONS

My father dropped out of school at a very early age. He was not very successful in school and thought it would be better to find a job to help his sister, who was raising him, pay the bills. He did whatever he could to bring a few dollars into the house, despite his sister's protests and desire for him to go back to school. He eventually became a delivery boy for a local grocery store. He would deliver groceries purchased by customers in a push cart. Yes, this was in the 1930's when walking was a much more common occurrence than today in many communities that make up our nation. My father had a number of labor intensive type jobs all of his life. Most of them had something to do with deliveries. His last job, before retiring due to heart problems, was as a furniture delivery man for a small family owned department store. He held this particular job for over thirty years.

Well my father married my mother at the age of nineteen. By twenty-six he had five children, four by my mom, and enough money saved to purchase a car. By the way, I was not yet born. My dad had to secure a driver's license before he could legally drive. The eye examination became a life changing event for my dad. It was at this time that my dad found out that he needed glasses! After getting his first pair of glasses my father realized something very significant. What was once thought of as a learning deficiency was now realized as a seeing issue. My father could not read well while in school because of poor vision! His glasses helped him see much better, gave him more self-confidence and caused him to become a lover and debater of the printed word.

I remember coming home one day after school super excited. I had something to tell my dad about my day at school. When he came home I told my dad about this big trailer full of books that stopped by my elementary school. My teacher took the class out to the bookmobile and I was amazed at all of the books inside. We had a library at school, but it was so small compared to this bookmobile. I told my mom and dad everything that I knew, and thought that I knew, about the bookmobile. The bookmobile had about four times as many books in it than our tiny library at school. Most of the books, unlike the ones in the school library, looked in great shape, even new! I told my mom and dad that I quickly looked through books and saw no torn pages. Most of the books in the school library had at least a few torn pages. Most of the pages were white too, not yellowish brown like the ones in the school library.

All of those books were so mesmerizing and made me very excited. I told my parents that I planned on reading every book in that bookmobile. So the very next Saturday my father took me to the local library branch, which was actually quite a ways away from our apartment, and registered me for a library card. I had never seen so many books in one place! All of those books; how could I read all of them? Well, my father told me to walk to this library and check out books every two weeks. He set aside thirty minutes most week nights when I read from a book and he, usually, read a newspaper. We would then talk about what we read and what it meant to us. My father always managed to question my thinking in ways that caused me to be prepared to defend whatever position that I took. To prepare, I had to think about the counter arguments. I had to imagine outcomes. Oh I had so much fun preparing to counter my father's comments with alternatives that now seem so fanciful and illogical at times. These debates were also common when we discussed sports.

My father would tell me, the youngest and only child left at home at the time, "If you can read and comprehend what you are reading, then no one can ever stop you from learning." This very positive and factual message is now part of my core being. The evenings of reading and discussing with my dad helped me see the world outside of my little bubble. The discussions caused me to ponder the possibilities, figuring out ways to make possibilities reality, and then making it so. These discussions caused me to think more deeply about things in order to justify my statements. They also caused me to realize that I could live a life in the future that was much better that the set of my current experiences, in my immediate surroundings. I wonder if my father knew how our time together helped to empower me to use my critical thinking skills in everything that I do and to purposely surround myself with like-minded individuals.

I believe that most, if not all, individuals have the ability to think about issues in complex ways. Most of us can develop options to address questions and concerns that are important to our lives. We can also make decisions that we believe represent the best actions to take to address these questions and concerns. Becoming more of a critical thinker empowers one to:

- self-analyze themselves;
- develop a better sense of self;
- make more informed and better decisions more often;
- channels thoughts towards social advocacy; and
- enhances leadership skills.

Finally, growing up humane and decent people who can appreciate others and take satisfaction in doing things well requires schools that model humanity and decency, that cultivate appreciation, and that support learning about things that matter to the people in them. Education should be a source of nurturance for the spirit as well as a means of reaching understanding, though it can be, and too often is, conducted in a way that deadens and demoralizes. Tedious, coercive schooling creates frustrations that must emerge sooner than later in self-deprecation, despair, or violence against others. However, where a real connection is made between students and teachers in the pursuit of meaningful accomplishments, the possibilities for developing lifelong capacities for learning, doing, and relating to others are greatly expanded (Darling-Hammond, 1997, p. 31).

The engaged leader works to create a teaching and learning environment where critical thinking is encouraged instead of suppressed. She/he fosters an atmosphere of 'what if.' Thoughts and actions are focused on ways to expand the success of the enterprise. Enhancing facilities, identifying new teaching techniques, finding better ways to motivate the learner all become ways of thinking that creates high levels of excitement and positive energy. The leader is actively engaged in these and other conversations, followed by action, with stakeholders. These conversations take place in informal and formal settings, in large and small groups or one to one, all initiated by anyone with an idea. Yet more common are the environments that reward compliance instead of creativity. I want to share an example regarding how critical thinking is often suppressed in our schools.

Suppression of critical thinking often emerges from decisions that were designed to help improve the teaching and learning process. Once recognized, a process that impedes instead of empowers must be changed. For example, there are basically two methods to initially assess an individual. One approach, referred to here as the deficit model, tends to try to determine what the individual does not know. The other approach tries to build on the gifts of the individual. The following scenario brings clarity to the both approaches to teaching and learning, and the outcomes that often result.

The local school district has experienced an increase in student enrollment over the past three years. Most of the increase has occurred due to the growth of both Mong and Salvadorian neighborhoods on the outer boundaries of the school district. A drop in academic performance, as measured by the state, has raised concerns. Concerns have caused district leaders to focus on determining the most appropriate way to teach these students. So, the district approved a policy that called for the administration of a readiness test to be given to elementary school students registering for the first time.

The test, each claimed by district official to be age appropriate, was designed to determine if a child was ready to take on the standard curriculum that the district has to offer its students. If a child does not score at a certain level on this test, they are placed in remedial, what students now call pre-prison, classes. There is really no need to go into all of the aspects of the test. The issue here is that the outcomes of this deficit model approach, as with most of them, results in less than adequate student growth. Remedial and back to the basics instructional methods seldom move beyond rote learning processes with memorization often being the optimal results. This type of teaching and learning seldom challenge the learner to think. Instead, they are simply taught, at best, to memorize. This deficit model approach, designed to determine if a child is ready to take on one way of teaching, much like other standardize test, simply tells us, to some extent, what a person knows. Deficit model testing does little to help us better understand how each learner learns. We must all understand that all can and do learn!

Deficit Model test become a tool to track learners. The results are often used to determine who will be prepared for college and a career, who will be prepared to graduate from high school and get a job, and who will be forced out of high school, often leading to spending some time in prison. Often, due to the perceptual barriers regarding learning deficiencies these students are seldom afforded teaching and learning environments that help to empower them to learn how to learn for themselves. Some people simply believe that certain individuals have limited abilities to think critically. What a shame!

We can provide the kinds of teaching and learning environments that help to empower learners learn how to learn for themselves. However, we must believe in the learner's capacity to do so. Deficit Model testing results in deficit model approaches to teaching and learning. We must jettison deficit model testing. The task here is to clearly understand that we all have gifts; we all can learn; and we all can make positive contributions to our families, organizations, society and for ourselves. The belief in the potential of the learner versus a deficit model approach is something the engaged leader must embrace and believe.

It is strongly suggested here that teaching and learning is maximized when students are afforded opportunities to take ownership; when they become their own teachers; when they grow in their abilities to learn how to learn for themselves. The same set of premises hold true with adults. Worker productivity is maximized when individuals are afforded opportunities to take ownership, when they can voice their opinions, and when their thoughts are turned into actions that lead to higher levels of success within the organization. I do not know if he knew it, but this is what my father did for me. My father helped to empower me to imagine, think, and learn. My life has been dedicated to help empower others to imagine, think and learn how to learn for themselves.

School leaders often use similar deficit models to determine the abilities and value of individual staff members. For example, an individual may have had little to no experience exploring questions that lead to more informed and better solutions. Initially this person may seem to lack the ability to engage in a series of discussions of such depth. However, when the leader believes that we all have the ability to learn, even when initially they do not know, his/her approach is focused on the possibilities instead of perceived deficits.

It is posited here that engaged and empowered teachers/leaders will result in engaged and empowered learners/staff and future leaders. In other words this culture, built on a foundation of possibilities, leads to an organizational climate full of potential and positive results. Imagining the possibilities of what can happen, and then setting into place the action steps to make it so, diminishes the perceptual barriers of deficit model thinking. This culture of possibilities, reinforced through a free flow of conversations, empowers all stakeholders to focus on what each can do to improve their work and the success of the organization.

REFERENCES

Darling-Hammond (1997). The Right To Learn: A Blueprint For Creating Schools That Work. San Francisco: Jossey-Bass.

CHAPTER 9

TODAY'S PUBLIC SCHOOLS

A Need for Change

TRANSFORMATION BY RONALD FERGUSON

I started kindergarten
Two or three steps behind.
Some classmates understood things
That had never crossed my mind.
Now that there's a new prescription
For the way our school is run,
Everbody's got new goals to reach,
It's getting to be fun!
The kids who looked real different
Seemed so smart (I can recall).
Kids who looked and spoke like I did
Didn't seem so smart at all.
We're learning to get smarter
'Cause our teachers show us how.
They're all serious about it.
Everyone's important now!
Of course there were exceptions,
But on mostly any day,
It was clear those kids were doing best
And we were just okay.
Time in class is so exciting
That we seldom fool around.
We might make a joke in passing,
But we quickly settle down.
Our teachers liked them better
'Cause they always knew the answers,
So kids like me just tried to be
Good athletes and great dancers.
After school we do our homework.
Often in our study groups.
When we need them we have tutors
And they give us all the "scoops."

The years went by quite slowly
And most things just stayed the same,
Until our principal decided
It was time to change the game.
If there's something that's confusing,
It's a temporary thing
'Cause the teachers love to answer
All the questions that we bring.
She hinted that the reason
When those others kids did best
Was that many knew already
More of what was on the tests.
All the counselors and teachers
Work with parents as team
'Cause they share the same commitment
To connect us with our dreams.
They learned it from their parents
And from things they did at home.
Much that I and my companions
Never had the chance to know.
I love the way things are now.
It all just seems so right!
We still play sports and we're still cool,
But now we're also "bright."
That had always been the pattern.
Yes for years it was the same.
But the standards movement came along
To finally change the game.
That first day of kindergarten
Some of us were way behind.
But today I'm graduating
In a truly different time.

CHRISTOPHER POOLE

Christopher officially stopped going to school when he was sixteen years old. He basically thought that school was a huge waste of time. It was also demoralizing. After-all Chris cannot remember a time when he even enjoyed going to school. His mom will tell you that Chris was eager to attend school when he was little, but that enthusiasm diminished with each year of attendance.

> Teachers tried to tell me what to do all day at school. There was no freedom. Man they treated us like slaves. They would tell me when to line-up and sit-down. Teachers would tell me to stop talking; stop singing to myself; stop moving in my seat; stop hitting people; and just stop, stop, stop! They even told me when to use the toilet and when to eat. I didn't pay much attention to the teachers at school when I did go. I mean, they showed us no respect. They treated all of us like criminals. We all felt like we were in lock-down. It was almost like they were preparing us for prison life! School was one of the worst places to be. Even the crazy stuff going on in the neighborhood was easier to deal with than the rules at school. At least I could earn some respect in my neighborhood. I started spending more time hanging out and avoiding the police than going to school. I could be me in the streets. I could be a man.

> I have never listened to anyone, including my mom, so why should I listen to all of these women at school? So I kept doing whatever I felt like doing, almost.

> I got time-outs, then infractions, and suspensions. They even took my mother to teen court and gave her a ticket. Nothing stopped me from doing what I wanted to do. I was finally suspended when I was in middle school pending a hearing, but we were never told when the hearing would take place. So I kind of just stopped going to school. Instead I just did more forty's and weed, and whatever my mom and her boyfriends left around the apartment. I had some friends and so we would steal a little or snatch a purse to get a little cash. We even robbed a few stores or broke into a house when we got bored. I got used to getting put in jail. Just some more people trying to tell me what to do.

During my days as a public school principal, I would remind teachers that our students wanted to feel good about themselves. I would tell teachers that our students wanted to feel a sense of accomplishment. Just like all people, they all wanted to be good at something. If they were not successful in their classwork, they would find ways to be successful disrupting the class. I would always say, "Student's actions are often reactions to adult behavior." If our students thought that they were loved, treated fairly, and really could learn, then they would reciprocate in-kind. The opposite was also true.

Public schools, especially ones in urban environments, are full of students who react in ways similar to Christopher when the process of teaching and learning fails to recognize the need to address the whole student. They learn to hate the daily doses of drill and rote teaching techniques employed by their teachers. These students learn to hate the structure in these schools and feel invisible. The systematic, timeline controlled, dehumanizing process do not afford students with opportunities to internalize new information. Teachers simply request a regurgitation of basic facts. This way of teaching and learning discourages real discussions in the classroom. It diminishes changes to develop the kinds of critical, reflective thinking needed for tomorrow's leaders. The process reminds one of an assembly line where information is downloaded on to inanimate objects at each stop (grade). Our students deserve more, much more.

> The schools we envision are exciting places; thoughtful, reflective, engaging, and engaged. They are places where meaning is made. They are places that resemble workshops, studios, galleries, theaters, studies, laboratories, field research sites, and newsrooms. Their spirit is one of shared inquiry. The students in these schools feel supported in taking risks and thinking independently. They are engaged in initiating and assessing their ideas and products, developing a disciplined respect for their own work and the work of others. Their teachers function more like coaches, mentors, wise advisors, and guides than as information transmitters or gatekeepers. They offer high standards with high levels of support, creating a bridge between challenging curriculum goals and students' unique needs, talents, and learning styles. They are continually learning because they teach in schools where everyone would be glad to be a student, or a teacher – where everyone would want to be – and could be – both.
>
> Darling-Hammond, 1997, pg. xiv.

LEARNERS

Education in the types of schools described in the quote above believe that most, if not all, students have the ability, desire and right to learn. They understand that learning occurs in multiple ways, and in a variety of settings. These teaching and learning environments find multiple ways to facilitate a process that enhances each student's own capacity for learning. Students become empowered to learn for themselves. Active engagement in the teaching and learning a process is utilized as an essential tool for understanding. Students, in these schools, know that they can, and do learn. They take ownership of their learning and growth. These students are excited about their experiences in these schools and are indeed becoming well prepared to successfully live, work and provide leadership with all kinds of individuals, anywhere in the world.

Yet our public school systems today, except in some suburban, magnet, and school within school settings, are much different than what is described in the quote above by Linda Darling-Hammond. Leaders in today's public school environments face what Joel Spring, and others, describe as top down bureaucratic structures, with system-wide state mandated curricula, and using high-stakes testing to measure student, teacher and administrator success. It is also used to close schools deemed unsuccessful and the loss of employment. These are the kinds of schools where many students learn to hate to attend.

The bureaucratic organization of these new school systems was made up of the following elements:

- A hierarchy with a superintendent at the top and orders flowing from the top to the bottom of the organization.
- Clearly defined differences in roles of superintendent, principals, assistant principals, and teachers.
- Graded schools in which students progressively moved from one grade to another.
- A graded course of study for the entire school system to assure uniformity in teaching in all grades in the system.
- An emphasis on rational planning, order, regularity, and punctuality.

Spring, 2011, pg. 68.

This system has evolved into and is moving towards a greater nationalization of school policies and more centralization of decision making, with high levels of pressure from the political and business sectors, regarding what, who and how students will be taught. Gaining momentum with the 1983 report, 'A Nation at Risk,' politicians and business sector leaders have charged that our public schools were failing and in need of major change. Since then the information delineated from these sectors of our society tells the general public that our public schools are failing and that these failures are putting the nation at risk in the global economy.

The philosophical premise that seemed to dominate this call for change reminds one of an essentialist approach. Educators supporting essentialism support the premise that there is a common core of knowledge that needs to be transmitted to student in a systematic, disciplined way. Emphasis is placed on intellectual and moral standards that schools should teach. Lecture is the most common form of teaching, with students as passive, submissive learners. The core of curriculum is essential knowledge and skills and academic rigor geared towards the memorization of facts. However, the focus is on the basics – reading, writing, speaking and computing clearly and logically. This form of education has resulted in classrooms focused on rote memorization; drill baby drill! Thoughtful, reflective and engaging activities are seldom, if ever utilized in these settings.

Many scholars, for example Finn and Ravitch, Berliner and Biddle, have shared data demonstrating that our schools are failing and placing the nation at risk. However, the movement for more accountability and structure within our public schools gained the kind of momentum that resulted in the 2001 federal legislation, "No Child Left Behind."

No Child Left Behind sought to close the achievement gap between rich and poor students by creating common curriculum standards, closing failing schools, and the public reporting of student test scores.

Spring, 2011, pg. 36.

This piece of federal legislation, formally called the Elementary and Secondary Education Act, has led to more teachers teaching in ways that result in the rote memorization of information that is included in mandated test. Teaching and learning environments lack an atmosphere for student risk-taking, students thinking critically about newly learned information, and for any reflective and/or research based activities. Opportunities to ask shy, think more critically and develop the skills for self-directed learning have almost disappeared in many public school settings. Teachers and administrators have circled the wagons. They have moved into survival mode in attempts to raise test scores, avoid public scorn, and save their jobs. I would suggest to you that the process of teaching and learning that is designed to get a certain percentage of students to pass a test is unjust, even criminal. When looking at the mis-education of so many of our children in today's public schools, one wonders if there is a correlation between these actions and the growth of the prison industry in our great nation. Much of the blame for this deplorable process of teaching and learning in today's public schools can be traced back to the changes that have resulted in too much state and federal control of the educational process. Our private schools, for the most part, know better. They continue to connect with their students by creating exciting places where meaning is learned and made. Students in these settings are motivated and actively engaged in the teaching and learning process.

Yet, as I have said before, we know that this type of teaching and learning environment is designed more to insure that there is a workforce that is willing to follow and not question leadership. It is a process utilized to control the percentage of students actually attending and graduating from four year colleges and universities. The preference here is to ensure that we have more followers, in lower paying jobs, than leaders, in higher paying jobs, as a way to control the masses and avoid chaos.

> As education is reduced to a mindless infatuation with metrics and modes of testing, the space of public schooling increasingly enforces this deadening experience with disciplinary measures reminiscent of prison culture. Moreover, as the vocabulary and disciplinary structures of punishment replace education, a range of student behaviors are criminalized resulting in the implementation of harsh mandatory rules that push many students deeper into the juvenile or adult criminal justice system…Removed from the normative and pedagogical framing of classroom life, teachers no longer have the option think outside of the box, to experiment, be poetic, or inspire joy in their students. They no longer have the freedom or power to teach, as W.E.B. Du Bois poetically states "to learn to communicate with the stars."
> Henry Giroux: Education in the Crisis of Public Values: Challenging the Assault on Teachers, Students, & Public Education – 2012, Pg. 3.

TERRI MADISON

Terri Madison became a high school mathematics teacher two years ago. She graduated with undergraduates, as a double major, in Engineering and Teacher

Education with an emphasis in Secondary Mathematics. Terri also secured a graduate degree in Teacher Education before starting her career. Her parents suggested a career in engineering, in her father's firm, due to her success in the field. They also knew that she would make much more money as an engineer. But Terri loved learning. She loved figuring out new ways to answer questions, solve problems, and conduct scientific research. Terri wanted to share her excitement and love for learning with other, younger learners. She really thought they too would learn to love math.

While growing up in what most would consider an upper middle class home, Terri wanted to work with students from low income homes and in inner-city public schools. She saw a career in education as more than a job. A career in education would be her ministry. This work, she believed, would be her way of giving back and serving those less fortunate.

Terri's school observations, field experiences and actual internships were quite rewarding to her. She thought that she was successful connecting with the students in the schools that partnered with the college. Yes, the schools were both public and private, but they were also composed of students representing great diversity, including internationals. Terri was able to create teaching and learning activities, during her internship in particular, that even impressed her mentoring teachers. She used her creativity and knowledge about the students to really get them engaged, excited and more successful. Students worked in teams to identify and solve problems. They discussed and explored the various ways each group addressed the problems and how they came up with their answers. After some discussions, students found other, better ways to solve the math problems. Of course each math problem was tied to issues of interest to the students. Terri knew that this was the career for her. She really wanted to become an excellent master teacher. Terri's mentor teachers and her professors thought that she was indeed well prepared to join the ranks of professional teachers.

Terri accepted a position as a mathematics teacher at a high school in the big city school district back near her suburban home town. This particular high school had a history of challenges including low morale, gangs, and serious disciplined issues. In addition, students had historically scored very low on state mandated test.

Terri initially thought that she could make a difference as a teacher in this high school. She truly believed that her style of teaching would get her students actively engaged, and academically more successful. What Terri initially failed to realize was that the design of the curriculum and the timeline that was mandated did not allow her to implement any of her creative ideas. Every lesson was highly structured by some unknown group at the district level. All teachers in this school district were required to follow each lesson, step by step. Not only were the students bored, Terri and other teachers were too! Over the past two years the high school experienced no appreciable gains on the state mandated test. As a matter of fact, the only measurable increases were experienced in disciplinary infractions, failure rates, and teacher turnover. After much reflection and consultation with trusted family and friends, Terri has now decided to quit teaching, get married and become a stay at home mom.

Numerous teachers enter the field of education in our public inner city schools with thoughts and dreams similar to Terri. Unfortunately, most of them live nightmares instead of experiencing the fulfillment of those dreams. The system is broken. We have moved teaching away from being a profession. Teacher proof lesson plans have dump down the teaching and learning process. Teachers in these schools are required to read at students, ask students basic questions, and accepting only yes or no, either – or, answers from students and managers for crowd control. Now is the time to reverse these terrible trends. Now is the time to right the ship. Now is the time to allow professional teachers to do their jobs!

Teachers

Based on the quote from Darling-Hammond, one will note that teachers in these types of schools are also excited about their work. The teaching and learning environment demonstrates a high value for their abilities to make professional decisions in support of their students and school. These teachers set the stage for learning. They help to guide students by providing more questions than answers. The teaching and learning environment rewards risk-taking and finding new ways to increase understanding, and new knowledge. Activities in these classrooms cause learners to go well below the surface level of answers leading to deeper meaning and understanding. The energy created in these teaching and learning environments causes most, if not all, teachers in these schools to challenge themselves daily by actively taking part in learning activities. Learning activities include workshops, conferences, and learning from the other learners and teachers in the classroom, their students.

Oh, if only this depiction of our teachers were true. I believe that most, if not all, teachers enter the profession with these images of teaching and learning. However they quickly find that public school structures are not conducive to real teaching and learning. State and federal policies and procedures demand that teachers follow set curricula and timelines. They are pulled away from the types of teaching and learning environments that have proven to work in other, often private and magnet, school settings.

> The concerns of the teachers in our study are precisely those that current school reform efforts are seeking to address, yet many policies unwittingly set up greater prescriptions, which actually undermine the goals they seek. Few policy makers have undertaken the geological dig necessary to reverse the bureaucratic mandates that have piled up over the last hundred years. As a consequence, teachers and students find themselves trapped in catch-22 situations where they are asked to respond to new goals for schooling but are simultaneously caught in a web of rules, regulations, structures, and directives that directly and indirectly make it difficult, and in some cases impossible, to achieve those goals.
>
> Darling-Hammond, 1997, pg. 94.

There is often little to no room for any teacher creativity or autonomy. Opportunities to connect new information with the knowledge each students have internalized is almost non-existent. What a shame! Teachers in many of these public school settings are charged with simply transmitting basic information to students, time after time, after time, until a certain percentage has memorized it. It is no wonder that so many entering the profession of teacher education leave within three to four years, or less. One should only look at current situations to understand why potential pre-service teachers choose other career fields.

The system is broken. Our attempts to educate the masses just do not work. Educating those in upper income private schools, and even the top ten percent or so in other learning institutions has experienced much better academic results. However, for some reason, we choose to try other, less proven, methods to educate the masses. Some would argue that this tiered education process is purposely in place to support our free enterprise, democratic form of government. While a free enterprise, democratic form of government sound promising for all, rules have been in place to provide advantages for some, but not for most. From our very origins, one will quickly note that only land owners could vote!

After-all, if all students were prepared to successfully matriculate through college, who would be left to perform jobs requiring manual labor. Who has as their dream job the hope of cleaning restrooms in the shopping malls, picking up paper along the nation's highways, or collecting garbage in front of our homes, in all kinds of weather? Our system of education limits career choices by using proven failed techniques for educating people to think and take ownership of their learning. The system, it is argued by some, is actually very successful. It is successful, they say, because the hidden curriculum is designed to make followers out of the masses. This way the masses are easier to trick, bamboozle, and control. The masses then become happy just to have a job. They are no longer a threat to the elite and their children. They are not prepared to disturb the existing status quo.

LEADERSHIP

Leadership in the teaching and learning environments described here values the thoughts, opinions and expertise of the students, teachers, staff, parents and all of the other stakeholders impacting the school. Leaders in these schools understand the value of diverse perspectives. They work to make sure that all voices have maximum opportunities to participate as the schools strive to meet and exceed stated goals. The primary work of leadership in this type of environment is that of facilitator. Leadership becomes a facilitator of the educational process by clearing the pathway of teaching and learning. They remove the barriers and other obstacles thus allowing teachers and students to create environments that maximize growth in thinking and learning. They also embrace the role of teacher and learner by participating with/ like others in school activities. These engaged leaders also understand the value of learning outside of the traditional classroom walls. Experiences that help to connect prior knowledge with new information become a powerful tool in these school settings. The mission, values and core values of the school are lived each day.

They become actions that demonstrate the value of all of the gifts of each individual involved in a culture of inclusion.

The report, 'A Nation at Risk' was reported to the public and became the focal point of discussion regarding public education while I was completing requirements for administrator certification in Texas. The State of Texas, informed by Governor White's Blue Ribbon Commission lead by Ross Perot, published its own report on education reform in 1984. As a result, the Texas legislature passed House Bill 72. This legislation required, among other things, the statewide testing of students, and teachers. Test scores were made public, with the last high school examination, which could be taken several times after their senior year, determining whether or not a student received a high school diploma, or just a certificate of attendance. School districts across the state scrambled to meet these new state requirements for public school education. Teachers were even required to take a state mandated test, with failure eventually leading to decertification. The era of accountability through assessment started with a bang in Texas.

After serving as an elementary school assistant principal for two years, I became an elementary school principal, serving approximately 1,100 students and a staff of well over one hundred. The school was in the inner city and had scored among the lower five percent, in the state, on state mandated test the previous year. This school had a history of high teacher turn over, about one-third each year. It was in an area of high in crime. We had to deal with a great deal of criminal activity on and around the campus.

This particular school was two miles north of the school where I served as an assistant principal. We often worked with some of the same students as their parents moved from one apartment to the next – and back again. So I was very familiar with the students, parents, neighborhood and the challenges before us. This school was in trouble. It could go nowhere but up.

The Texas Educational Agency (TEA) had placed the school on some sort of warning status and was scheduled to send a contingent of educators to review our plan for improvement and to query the staff during the first month of the academic year. We had very little time to plan for this visit and develop our plan. Of course the district had a standard plan developed for us and the other failing schools. However, I privately felt that the plan was flawed. We needed to do more, even if these actions were not to be a part of some public document. While we were required to follow the state and district mandated curriculum and timeline, my thoughts focused on finding ways to really connect with our students. By the way, students at the time were assessed at the elementary level in the third and fifth grades only. Three areas were assessed, reading, writing, and mathematics. The national call at the time was 'back to the basics'.

I refused to ask teachers to teach to the test as other schools were doing. We had many discussions prior to the start of school with teachers in these grade level and others considered leaders in the building. We continued these discussions prior to the TEA visit. Eventually we developed a plan that covered all of the required mandates.

We produced a set of promotional documents that were approved by the district and eventually the team representing the Texas Education Agency. This was our plan, on paper. In reality we developed and implemented a plan that challenged students to think; to ask why; allowed more risk taking; encouraged students to elaborate in ways that caused them to connect this new information with things that they already understood. This plan, we believed, would help students more as they grew both academically and socially. Our students began spending time with me in small groups to review and discuss their writing samples. While initially shaking in their boots, they began to look forward to being with their really weird principal, who came up with all of these wild and crazy ideas to write about. We sent our students on field trips, to places like the Science Place, Aquarium, Children's Theatre, Zoo, even Luby's restaurant. We even had a student run school newspaper, with reporters at every grade level and for other areas of interest. These were places many of our students had never visited. These extended learning experiences were frowned upon by district officials. They believed that our students needed as much drill as possible in order to improve test scores. We developed a reward system, giving classes opportunities to earn free dessert during lunch. Rewards were based on many things. For example, when students left campus for any event I would randomly pick a student and ask them to tell me about their trip and share all that the group learned. After their return and my discussion with that student, I would announce over the public address system all that that class had learned based on my visit with the student. I would then announce free dessert for the entire class! Students just loved to be recognized in this way. Basically we just made learning fun. We expanded their world and showed them how others lived their lives. Students began to better understand that they too could live in different ways; that they could live in areas where shootings did not occur every night; and that they could have professional career instead of a series of low paying jobs. I could go on. Our students began to take pride in their accomplishments. Each year, more students became excited about school and really loved learning.

Teachers also decided to hang in with us. By the third year our only vacancies were due to retirements. Now I must also say that while our test scores increased each year, gains were not as dramatic as other schools in the area with similar demographics. I was once asked by my immediate supervisor why our gains did not reach the forty to fifty percent levels as some of the other schools. I immediately suggested that he visit the area middle school. I asked him to talk with the administrators and teachers to clearly see which students were performing at the highest levels and served as the majority of student leaders at the school. During our next meeting he stated that he no longer had concerns regarding our test gains. As I explained to him, we educated the whole child by helping them increase their own level of responsibility for learning each year. We help to instill not only a love for learning, but the necessity for becoming a learned citizen of this nation and world. Our students could think critically, debate, reflect and were gradually taking ownership of their own learning.

So yes, we can have better urban schools. However, it will take engaged leaders who are willing to walk, but not really cross, the line. It will take engaged leaders who truly practice inclusion in every aspect of the life of the school. A shift in educational philosophy is needed. We need to find support for more of a blend of educational philosophies that embrace the thinking of Progressivism and Reconstructionist.

Progressivism generally focused on the development of the whole child. This educational philosophy advocated this focus on the whole child and suggested we move away from a process focused on the content or the teacher. Educators supporting this philosophical approach thought that students should be able to explore ideas and concepts through active experimentation. A major questions approach to learning emerging from one's experiences should, they say, provide the foundation for learning. Learning here is active rather than passive. Students are problem solvers, critical thinkers, and originators of new understandings.

Reconstructionist, along with critical theorist to some degree, focused on the social questions. This work had as a major goal the creation of a better society and world, for everyone. Student experiences were wed to the social actions needed to successfully address the real problems of the world. The role of education was to prepare learners in ways that caused them to become agents for change and a new, better social order. I think that you can see the salient factors of these two educational philosophies embraced in the focus of this work. While components of other educational philosophies are also espoused in this work, the major direction finds its support in the work of progressive and reconstructionist ideology.

The kind of teaching and learning environment described by Darling-Hammond can exist. They do exist, despite the bureaucratic barriers along the pathway to success. Our challenge is to prepare and support more leaders willing to step up and lead to work that result in the kinds of engaged and inclusive teaching and learning environments that are the focus of this book.

REFERENCES

Darling-Hammond, Linda. (1997). The Right To Learn: A Blueprint for Creating Schools That Work. New York: Jossey-Bass.

Ferguson, Ronald. (2006). Transformation in A Small Flock of Poems for Teachers . http://www.dupage.k12.il.us/educators/Administrative_Leadership/pdf/DuPage,%20Ferguson%20Poems.pdf

Giroux, Henry. (2012). Education in the Crises of Public Values: Challenging the Assualt on Teachers, Students, & Public Education.

Spring, Joel. (2011). The Politics Of American Education. New York: Routledge.

Thomas, Cornell. (2004). Transgressing Culture Lines. Dubuque, Iowa: Kendall Hunt.

PREPARING TO BECOME AN ENGAGED LEADER

Learning from Failure

Management is not for the faint of heart. A career in management holds awesome responsibilities accompanied by the consequences of failure that can be far reaching. There are few jobs that provide a person with the opportunity to have a huge impact on the corporate bottom line by achieving results through the guidance and direction of others.

Carnes, K., Cottrell, D. and Layton, M. (2004). p. 82.

Thomas J. Watson is attributed with saying "If you want to succeed, double your failure rate". Wired Magazine editor Kevin Kelly likewise explains that a great deal can be learned from things going unexpectedly, and that part of science's success comes from keeping blunders "small, manageable, constant, and trackable". He uses the example of engineers and programmers who push systems to their limits, breaking them to learn about them. Kelly also warns against creating a culture (e.g. school system) that punishes failure harshly, because this inhibits a creative process, and risks teaching people not to communicate important failures with others.

Wikipedia

DREAMS

I use to think that I could make a difference. I would be able to change our community in significant ways. I would be able to help people see the value in other people. I really thought that this would happen. Multicultural, then diversity movements were just not enough. I thought that I could find a way that would allow those in power to journey into themselves. This journey would result in more people clearly understanding their own personal biases, the negative impact of these biases on others, and cause them to make needed change. I really thought that I could provide some focus, with others, to get this done.

I was not successful while serving as special assistant. Some would disagree and point to a legacy that has been institutionalized. We developed a program, The Community Scholar Program, which has had a tremendous impact on student diversity on campus. The academic success of students, overall grade point average, retention and graduation rates, in this program has also been exceptionable. The program provides scholarships to students from adopted high schools in the area.

The positive publicity about the program has also caused other students from diverse backgrounds to seek admission. While indeed the program represents a significant step towards a more inclusive community of learners, I would say that it is just not enough. We were also influential in the establishment of core courses designed to address issues of diversity and inclusion. The template designed to guide the development of these courses helped to move teaching and learning in this genre beyond the generalizations that typically exist at similar college courses throughout the country. The next step in the strategic plan called for the implementation of action steps designed to increase diversity within the ranks of the faculty and a series of optional professional development seminars for faculty and staff. Both initiatives failed to gain traction. A change in leadership and shift in priorities regarding the work of the office brought clarity to a decision I needed to make. Do I remain and just ride the wave of success regarding student diversity, relax and hope for a shifting of priorities done the road? After – all, new leadership verbally supported the work but just needed to shore up some areas first. Since I am not one to rest on past accomplishments, it was clear that it was time to move on. Or, do I realize that my time here was up and move on to other potential opportunities?

I joined the leadership team of another college as the first Systems Vice President for Institutional Diversity. Through some consolidation and the creation of some new positions, we were able to build a program that experienced high recognition form the president, trustees, and alumni. Our greatest success came from data that showed dramatic increases in the grade point average and retention rates of student minority groups. Our Inclusion Leadership program, consisting of students from all walks of life, was also seen as a great success. Both of these successful programs were supported with external funds. These funds were secured by my efforts. However, funding would not have materialized if the president had not continuously placed the work of diversity and inclusion one of his most important initiatives. However, the president soon left to take the same position in another state. We were making great progress towards building an infrastructure to solidify the work ahead, but the president who hired me left. The agenda loss support and the focus took a u-turn. So, I asked myself again: Do I remain and just ride the wave of success, or realize that my time here was up and move on to other potential opportunities? Since I was still not one to rest on passed accomplishments, it was clear that it was time to move one.

I thought that maybe I could make it happen at a small liberal arts college – as president. We would become an example of how a diverse and inclusive community of learners can impact thinking, beliefs, and actions in support of a better tomorrow. We developed a strategic plan to move the college forward in three key areas, academics, infrastructure, and financial sustainability. We made about four million dollars of improvements on the campus simply by redirecting existing revenue. After five years of budgets in the red, we righted the ship and achieved over a million dollars surplus in just three years. The other key initiative called for the strengthening of the student profile. Part of this initiative was addressed with the development of a new Honor's Program. This program consisted of a minor in Inclusion Studies. Courses were designed to attract a more diverse and better academically prepared group of students. Students successfully finishing this minor would be prepared to live, work, and provide leadership with all kinds of people – anywhere in the world. Trustees, during a conference call, voted to approve the program with no dissenting votes. However immediately after the conference call, the board chair called to say that he and four other trustees did not agree with this initiative. I was told that I just wanted smart students on campus and that I was moving to far away from the mission of the college. There was also push back on our desire to establish a more diverse student body to the college. An outline and list of courses are shared in Appendix A.

This small faction of the board of trustees, including the chair, could not see the vision; the dream; the pathway leading to a stronger, more diverse, and well recognized college; a place to be emulated. While other board members were very supportive of the work, I did not do a good enough job to convince this hand full of board leadership. So they, without the knowledge of many of the trustees and over the holiday season, removed me from office. A dream deferred, that indeed exploded.

So now I am back as a professor. I am still trying to make a difference. This time I am focused on my students, and possibly a few others. I am also trying to share some of my thoughts on the printed page. I am also working to establish the Center for Engaged Leadership. (The Center for Engaged Leadership is shared in Appendix D). Will this focus help students and others become better prepared as engaged leaders in a more diversely inclusive world? Will people read what I write, and take advantage of the programs offered by the Center, should it be established? Will these vehicles for teaching and learning about engaged leadership be strong enough to cause others to become stronger and more active agents for change? Will this work become one of the stronger voices focused on the movement towards engaged leadership and a true democracy?

For some reason, I have my doubts. However, I still have hope. I still believe that God is in control. I still believe that if it is God's will, then others will read, reflect, embrace, join, then place into action the changes needed to demonstrate that this country does indeed believe that all will be valued and included. We will become a community for all of humanity.

I want to believe that inclusion can become the norm in this country. I must believe, otherwise what is the use! One lesson learned is the fact that engaged leaders must focus on sustaining programs with long-term restricted financial support. Leaders come and go. Programs that remain are often ones with the kind of external financial support that serves as a buffer through the many changes in the life of a college or school. Endowed programs have a much better chance of sustainability. So I present these thoughts with the hope and prayer that you will see the value of engaged leadership. It is also my hope that you become active agents for change as we work to live up to our creed. "…and to the Republic for which it stands, one nation under God, indivisible, with Liberty and Justice for all." So, please read, reflect, discuss and make change. It will take all of us to make it so.

Amen

Like many other institutions, we have been working to develop new ways to educate our students to be flexible lifelong learners and leaders capable of responding to a world of constant change. We want to provide a foundation for intentional, critically engaged lifelong learners, people who can identify what they are learning and understand why it is relevant to their lives. We recognize that in order to learn for life, students will need to know how to consciously learn from their life experiences. They must learn how to pay attention to subtle "a-ha" moments, recognizing the insights and dissonance that often accompanies new learning. They will net to know how to work effectively within diverse teams and groups, balancing the needs and views of others while also staying engaged with their won intentions and sources of curiosity. To do this, they will need to be able to reflect critically on their decisions and actions, recognize the strengths and limitations of their own and others' perspectives, and continually seek feedback from others and the environment. This seems to be a tall order.

Peet, M. Reynolds-Keefer, L. Gurin, P. and Lonn, S. Fall 2011/Winter 2012.

Inclusion Studies Minor at _____ College

The Inclusion Studies Minor at _____ College is dedicated to educating learners about the importance of inclusion, diversity, and equity. All courses will engage each learner ways that will create opportunities for individuals to become more understanding, thoughtful, expressive, and intentional about the issues of inclusion, diversity, and equity. The courses in this minor will empower individuals towards a more personal sense of self-worth, cultural and personal histories, traditions, critical consciousness, and all that defines who we are. Focusing mostly on social, political, and economic issues that impact inclusion, diversity, and equity, learners will see that they are a part of a more inclusively diverse society. Comparative analysis regarding the impact of these issues will empower learners to better understand the world in which they live, and their role in making it a better place for everyone. Additional emphasis will be placed on actions we can take that will possibly lead to a more inclusively diverse world. A research component of the program will allow learners to answer their own questions ablutions inclusion, diversity and equity in uniquely personal ways.

Inclusion Studies courses and suggested sequence are shared on the following pages:

INCL 3323   THE IMPACT OF LABELS IN AMERICA

Course Description

This course will explore the meaning of being an American from various racial, gender, and ethnic perspectives. Emphasis will be placed on these perspectives from social, political, and economic points of view. Learners will also determine ways to become advocates for change – towards living what Dr. King and others call The Beloved Community.

Instructional Goals

The learner will develop a better understanding of what it means to be an American in the United States; has/does one's racial and/or ethnic background negatively impact these meanings of living as an American in America. In addition, the learner will seek answers to the question: Have all, Chicano, Italian, Sicilian, Polish, Latino, Arab, Asian, gender, GLBT, etc., groups been historically afforded the same opportunities as citizens in this great nation, and how can one help to make positive change?

Learning Outcomes

At the completion of this course the learner will demonstrate the ability to:

- articulate social generalizations used to describe a variety of racial, gender, and ethnic groups in the United States;
- share, orally and in writing, how racial, gender, and ethnic labels have resulted in barriers towards living the American Dream;
- organize groups to develop action steps with the goal to diminish and/or
- eliminate the negative impact of the labels placed on some citizens in the United States.

Methods of Instruction

The learner will be exposed to multiple perspectives regarding the questions posed in this course through readings, videos from multiple authors, class discussions, reflective practices (journaling, debating, and position papers), and active involvement in case study exercises.

Course Content

Professor Discretion

Course Evaluation

Learners will write a Statement of Purpose and Action paper in three segments. These segments will address the three learning outcomes listed in the course syllabus. Each segment, one every three weeks, will represent twenty percent of the final grade and can be improved throughout the semester. In addition, an oral and written presentation of all three parts of this paper will represent forty percent (twenty and twenty) of the final grade. This course will be taught over the first twelve weeks, four hours per week, of the semester.

INCL 3333   SOCIAL NETWORKING

Course Description

The term Social Networking in contemporary times is equivalent to networks on the world-wide web. However, as this course will examine, social networking involves a multitude of outlets and venues. By examining both the historical and current forms of social networking, the course will analyze an array of networking practices, who has access, and the influence it has on societal interaction, personal values, and trends. In addition, learners will explore the potential impact of social networking as advocates seek more equity in a future that supports notions of inclusion, among diversity.

Instructional Goals

The learner will develop a better understanding of the types of social networking sites being utilized most by individuals, how the use of sites are currently impacting individual ought, and how the use of these sites, and those in the future, can become tools for advocates seeking more equity and inclusion in our diverse world.

Learning Outcomes

At the completion of this course the learner will demonstrate the ability to:

- discuss in detail the use of various social networking sites;
- discuss the impact of social networking sites at it relates to the social, political, and economic impact regarding difference;
- develop ways to utilize social networking to promote the growth of a more inclusively diverse society.

Methods of Instruction

The learner will be exposed to multiple perspectives regarding the questions posed in this course through readings, videos from multiple authors, class discussions, reflective practices (journaling, debating, and position papers), and active involvement in case study exercises.

Course Content

Professor Discretion

Course Evaluation

Learners will write a Statement of Purpose and Action paper in three segments. These segments will address the three learning outcomes listed in the course syllabus. Each segment, one every three weeks, will represent twenty percent of the final grade and can be improved throughout the semester. In addition, an oral and written presentation of all three parts of this paper will represent forty percent (twenty and twenty) of the final grade. This course will be taught over the first twelve weeks, four hours per week, of the semester.

INCL 3343   THE POWER MOVEMENTS OF THE '60S

Course Description

This course will explore the power movements of the 1960s. It will examine this decade of peace and love – war and hate and the call for equality and sexual freedom. Specific attention will be given to the Vietnam War; Woodstock; King, Kennedy, Malcolm and Bobby; The Moon Landing; COINTELPRO and the Black Panther Movement; Baby Boomers; Chavez; Chisholm; Johnson; Race Riots; and The Beatles.

Instructional Goals

The learner will develop a better understanding of this decade's major power movements and the impact each has made on current social, political, and economic movements. Learners will seek ways to utilize this knowledge as each works to become advocates towards the development of a more inclusively diverse society in the United States, and the world.

Learning Outcomes

At the completion of this course the learner will demonstrate the ability to:

- articulate the impact of the various power movements of the 1960's discussed on people from varying backgrounds, from social, political, and economic perspectives;
- share, orally and in writing, the lessons learned from this study.

Methods of Instruction

The learner will be exposed to multiple perspectives regarding the questions posed in this course through readings, videos from multiple authors, class discussions, reflective practices (journaling, debating, and position papers), and active involvement in case study exercises.

Course Content

Professor Discretion

Course Evaluation

Learners will write a Statement of Purpose and Action paper in three segments. These segments will address the three learning outcomes list in the course syllabus. Each segment, one every three weeks, will represent twenty percent of the final grade and can be improved throughout the semester. In addition, an oral and written presentation of all three parts of this paper will represent forty percent (twenty and twenty) of the final grade. This course will be taught over the first twelve weeks, four hours per week, of the semester.

INCL 3353   GLOBALIZATION: IS THE WORLD REALLY FLAT?

Course Description

The World Wide Web and other forms of social media, the convergence of technology and the need for greed has transformed our work. We are now better able to communicate and know about the events of the world, almost as they occur. Corporate partnerships, global supply chain processes and instant messaging have impacted our lives, but in varying degrees. This course will explore how access to this new way of life has empowered some while virtually debilitating the lives of others. It will also discuss the negative impact of greed.

Course Instructional Goals

The learner will develop a better understanding of the impact that social media, technology, and business partnerships have had on the social, political, and economic issues faced in the United States and the world. The learner will also seek to bring clarity to the disparities between the issues of globalization and Americans from different walks of life.

Learning Outcomes

At the completion of this course the learner will demonstrate the ability to:

- articulate the impact of globalization on Americans from different walks of life from social, political, and economic perspectives;
- share, orally and in writing, then lessons learned from this study;
- organize groups tom develop action steps with the goal to provide equal access to the world of globalization to all Americans.

Methods of Instruction

The learner will be exposed to multiple perspectives regarding the questions posed in this course through readings, videos from multiple authors, class discussions, reflective practices (journaling, debating, and position papers), and active involvement in case study exercises.

Course Content

Professor Discretion

Course Evaluation

Learners will write a Statement of Purpose and Action paper in three segments. These segments will address the three learning outcomes listed in the course syllabus. Each segment, one every three weeks, will represent twenty percent of the final grade and can be improved throughout the semester. In addition, an oral and written presentation of all three parts of this paper will represent forty percent (twenty and twenty) of the final grade. This course will be taught over the first twelve weeks, four hours per week, of the semester.

INCL 4323 MUSIC, FILM, AND MEDIA – IT'S ALL IN THE WAY
ONE LOOKS AT THINGS

Course Description

Music, film, television, and media have influenced the way individuals think, believe, and act. This course will examine these influences as they relate to equity in a more diversity and inclusive society.

Course Instructional Goals

The learner will develop a better understanding of the impact music, film, television, and other media have on how an individual thinks, believe, and act. More specifically, the learner will seek to bring clarity to the messages sent through these media outlets and how the impact may vary with and within different groups of Americans.

Learning Outcomes

At the completion of this course the learner will demonstrate the ability to:

- articulate the impact that the various messages received through music, film, television and other media from social, political, and economic perspectives;
- share orally, and in writing, the lessons learned from this study;
- organize groups to empower others to learn how to block the negative impact of these messages and to promote messages that support the value of all people.

Methods of Instruction

The learner will be exposed to multiple perspectives regarding the questions posed in this course through readings, videos from multiple authors, class discussions, reflective practices (journaling, debating, and position papers), and active involvement in case study exercises.

Course Content

Professor Discretion

Course Evaluation

Learners will write a Statement of Purpose and Action paper in three segments. These segments will address the three learning outcomes listed in the course syllabus. Each segment, one every three weeks, will represent twenty percent of the final grade and can be improved throughout the semester. In addition, an oral and written presentation of all three parts of this paper will represent forty percent (twenty and twenty) of the final grade. This course will be taught over the first twelve weeks, four hours per week, of the semester.

INCL 4333   EDUCATION FOR SOCIAL CHANGE

Course Description

High-stakes testing, ACT, SAT, GRE and other normed testing practices are often utilized to determine a student's access to learning. Yet it is espoused by most that a quality education is critically important to success in the United States. This course examines historical and current efforts, and its impact to educate all Americans in the United States.

Course Instructional Goals

The learner will develop a better understanding of the education system(s) in the United States and the disparities between the quality of education provided to some citizens, but not all.

Learning Outcomes

At the completion of this course the learner will demonstrate the ability to:

- articulate the disparities in the educational system in the United States;
- share, orally and in writing, the lessons learned from this study;
- organize groups to equalize the teaching and learning process for all Americans.

Methods of Instruction

The learner will be exposed to multiple perspectives regarding the questions posed in this course through readings, videos from multiple authors, class discussions, reflective practices (journaling, debating, and position papers), and active involvement in case study exercises.

Course Content

Professor Discretion

Course Evaluation

Learners will write a Statement of Purpose and Action paper in three segments. These segments will address the three learning outcomes listed in the course syllabus. Each segment, one every three weeks, will represent twenty percent of the final grade and can be improved throughout the semester. In addition, an oral and written presentation of all three parts of this paper will represent forty percent (twenty and twenty) of the final grade. This course will be taught over the first twelve weeks, four hours per week, of the semester.

INCL 4343   THE GOSPEL AND SOCIAL CHANGE

Course Description

The Gospel is proclaimed as the truth, the way, and the light. Yet the interpretation of the Gospel has often been used to uplift some while vilifying others. This course will explore interpretation of the Gospel and its impact on Americans from social, political, and economic perspectives.

Course Instructional Goals

The learner will develop a better understanding of the Christian Gospel and how messages have historically been used in ways that have supported the actions of some Americans, at the expense of others. The learner will also seek to bring clarity to why disparities exist between the written Gospel and the interpretations of respected theologians.

Learning Outcomes

At the completion of this course the learner will demonstrate the ability to:

• articulate the impact of the varying interpretations of the Gospel on people from varying walks of life, from social, political, and economic perspectives;
• share, orally and in writing, the lessons learned from this study;
• organize groups to develop action steps with the goal to bring forth the truth of the Gospel for all who desire to hear.

Methods of Instruction

The learner will be exposed to multiple perspectives regarding the questions posed in this course through readings, videos from multiple authors, class discussions, reflective practices (journaling, debating, and position papers), and active involvement in case study exercises.

Course Content

Professor Discretion

Course Evaluation

Learners will write a Statement of Purpose and Action paper in three segments. These segments will address the three learning outcomes listed in the course syllabus. Each segment, one every three weeks, will represent twenty percent of the final grade and can be improved throughout the semester. In addition, an oral and written presentation of all three parts of this paper will represent forty percent (twenty and twenty) of the final grade. This course will be taught over the first twelve weeks, four hours per week, of the semester.

INCL 4353   CAPSTONE RESEARCH PROJECT

Course Description

Research provides a vehicle to raise and answer questions that are important to us. This course will provide research techniques to answer personal questions related to equity, inclusion and diversity.

Course Instructional Goals

The learner will research a personal issue of equity, diversity and inclusion that is impacting his/her life using ethnographic research technology. This research will bring clarity to the questions being asked and create a pathway of action steps that will help the researcher, and others, as we work in support of equity in a more inclusively diverse society.

Learning Outcomes

At the completion of this course the learner will demonstrate the ability to:

*   successfully conduct ethnographic research;
*   use research results to formulate action steps designed to address the findings.

Methods of Instruction

The learner will be exposed to multiple perspectives regarding the questions posed in this course through readings, videos from multiple authors, class discussions, reflective practices (journaling, debating, and position papers), and active involvement in case study exercises.

Course Content

Professor Discretion

Course Evaluation

Learners will write a Statement of Purpose and Action paper in three segments. These segments will address the three learning outcomes listed in the course syllabus. Each segment, one every three weeks, will represent twenty percent of the final grade and can be improved throughout the semester. In addition, an oral and written presentation of all three parts of this paper will represent forty percent (twenty and twenty) of the final grade. This course will be taught over the first twelve weeks, four hours per week, of the semester.

The _____ Center for Engaged Leadership
    Great leaders throughout history discovered the power of connection to inspire people to superior performance, individually and collectively. Employee engagement soars in Connection Cultures where everyone feels like a part of the team.

E PLURIBUS PARTNERS

Introduction

Parker Palmer, Luis Cabrera, Thomas Friedman, Jim Collins, Tom Slone and Max Depree represent authors recently espousing the need for future leaders with the abilities to work successfully with people from all walks of life. They express the need for individuals who have the ability to think in more complex ways, listen intently to the thoughts of others, and to make the kind of connections between individuals to move an organization forward in dynamically successful ways. These kinds of connections help to empower individuals to see the connections between their attributes and desires with the goals of the organization. Glickman's premise of a cause beyond self permeates the culture of the organization.

Description of the Concept

Many of us grew up from childhood learning to understand, for example, right from wrong, good or bad, smart or dumb, strong or weak, pretty or ugly, acceptance or rejection. Sharing was a right thing to do, while selfishness was bad. Following directions from your parents and teachers was a good thing to do, but hitting your sibling was bad. You were rewarded for the smart things that you did, and punished for your actions that were considered dumb. Mather strongest person won the trophy, the weakest got dirt kicked in their face. Those considered pretty (handsome) got all of the attention, while those considered ugly would be marginalized most all the time. If you were considered good, then you were accepted by those in control. All others were deemed different and not included in the inner circles of the main group.
    These straightforward examples of treatment based on either/or descriptors are at the root of many of the ills of our society today. Seemingly basic, clear-cut ways of making sense of the world plague our attempts to value anyone that seems to be different. This approach has caused many of us in this society to think gays, racial groups, non-Christians, and those with a disability, for example, as less than. Thinking in this way has lead to a sense of alienation for so many citizens in this country and entitlement for others. What is most alarming is that differences are attributed to individuals based merely on socially constructed group identifiers. How do we right this ship? I believe that the _____ Center for Engaged

Leadership will provide one great pathway leading to better connections between individuals, and within themselves.

Key Actions

1. Seminars will provide the kinds of experiences, encounters and reflective opportunities that empower individuals toward a more personal sense of self worth, cultural and personal histories, traditions, critical consciousness, leadership, and all that defined who we are and how we are a part of a more inclusively diversity society.
   * Seminars will be specifically designed for, for example:
     School district administrators;
     School district faculty;
     Middle level business 1administrators and hiring managers;
     Not-for-profit organizations;
     Student organizations (college to middle school);
     Etc.
2. Research: the program will afford graduate students at TWC with the opportunity to answer their own questions about inclusion, leadership and connections in uniquely personal ways. They will develop their skills to facilitate this work in the center and in their careers.This work will empower participants to become advocates for change in support of a better, more connected global society.
3. Conference on Inclusion Studies
   An annual conference focused in engaged leadership, inclusion, and connections will provide a venue for:
   1. Participants to discuss and reflect on their perspectives;
   2. Leaders from corporate, government, university and other settings to discuss and reflect on their perspectives; and
   3. Companies to hire individuals better prepared for global leadership.

Outcomes

The _____Center for Inclusion Studies is dedicated to educating learners about the importance of inclusion and connections. The Center believes that:

1. Engaged pedagogy will challenge the learner intellectually and personally in ways that lead to more comprehensive perspectives;
2. Intellectually stimulating leadership, communication, research and outreach activities all lead to learners with highly developed connecting skills;
3. A high level of student-faculty interaction (in and outside of the formal classroom steering) leads to learners with the ability to critically analyze and better understand issues from a variety of view points;

4. The work will provide learners with the tools needed to demystify the ways in which issues of social stratification impact the ability to connect with others;
5. These activities will cause learners to become actively involved in diminishing the societal barriers that impede connections; and
6. The experience will lead to more individuals becoming proactive advocates for leadership focused connecting and including.

SUPPLEMENTAL ONE

Seminar Overview (Two Week Seminar in Washington, DC)

Cultural awareness has become, in many settings, the practice of acknowledging and respecting the various groups of people in our world. These generalized and often overly simplified depictions of culture homogenize groups of people and efface individuality and differences that are so important to our identities. The generalizations often become perceptual barriers as individuals attempt to provide leadership within their organizations and/or community. The kinds of relationships needed between individuals have little chance of developing to their full potential when these generalizations control our thoughts and actions. This seminar will broaden the cultural perspectives of students and equip them with ways to think about, discuss, and express more informed opinions regarding notions of culture. They will become better equipped as advocates for a better society and world.

The intellectual structure of the seminar will be developed through the use of a conceptual framework focusing on what might be called the "major Questions" approach. Human societies have had to be concerned both with the process of nurturing their citizens and with determining what would constitute the particular set of characteristics (intellectual and social) they should acquire in their development so that they might function efficaciously within the social institutions that mark that society.

An individual's preparation for life and leadership in a more globally diverse society may indeed consist of reflective processes to better understand who they are, why they think about others the way that they do, and how to make any needed change. Thus, it seems reasonable to assert that the "liberally educated person" should be provided with the educational opportunity to examine these issues in a deliberate, intensive, and sustained manner.

- The activities associated with the course should result in students who are:
- able to articulate major attributes that determine one's identity;
- conscious of the political, economic, and social-cultural factors that affect the issues/challenges;
- familiar with the philosophic perspectives that serve as the conceptual grounds for positions on such issues;
- able to analyze the issues/challenges and gain a clearer understanding of what is involved in such issues, including conceptual clarity of major ideas related to these issues, and familiarity with the major "positions" on such issues; and
- as a consequence of the analysis and critical scrutiny of these ideas and positions, students will be able to develop reasoned positions on these significant issues.

The "Major Questions: Leading to Engaged Leaders.

1. What are the major attributes that determine one's identity and why?
2. What are the political, economic, and social-cultural factors that impact one's thinking about differences among individuals?
3. Given the answers to the first two questions, how have your thoughts about diversity, inclusion and engaged leadership changed and how will your answers cause you to become a stronger advocate for a better society and world, for all?

TENTATIVE SCHEDULE OF ACTIVITIES

Week One
Day One
Introductions/Seminar Requirements/Topics: Identity & Leadership

Day Two
Site Visits: Morning and afternoon site visits to two leaders within organizations (to be determined), representing different perspectives on leadership and who they are as a leader and person.

Day Three
Reflecting on site visits/Case Study Applications/Writing Drafts on questions one.

Day Four
Philosophy of Diversity Questionnaire with discussion/Afternoon site visit with Chief Diversity Officer or Diversity Advocate (to be determined).

Day Five
Reflective group work (composing ideas focused on week's experiences and discussing in small groups for clarity and growth)/Question One Due by 4 PM.

*Paper will be emailed back to students over the weekend. Questions and readings regarding the political, economic, and social-cultural factors will also be sent as a introduction for Monday's bus tour.

Week Two
Day One
Bus tour of DC and surrounding area to compare social stratification issues. Lunch stop at organization (to be determined) with speaker to discuss issue and their work.

Day Two
Site Visits: Morning and afternoon site visits with two leaders within two organizations (to be determined), representing different (hopefully Democratic and Republican) perspectives regarding an approach to address the social stratification of our society. (Discussions will include economic and social-cultural factors).

Day Three
Reflecting on site visits/Case Study Applications/Writing Drafts on questions two.

Day Four

Work on completion of Philosophical Platform/One on One consultations with me/ Dinner celebration with community and TWC leaders/Presentation by selected speaker.

Day Five

Individual presentations of platforms with group discussion/leave for home after 1:00 PM/Platform Due by Monday 4 PM.

SUPPLEMENTAL TWO

BUILDING YOUR PLATFORM ON ENGAGED LEADERSHIP

What follows is an explanation of creating a Platform. I want to begin with two important considerations that should influence your writing.

- This Platform is yours, you are not explaining what all individuals should believe or do. You will be talking about your own beliefs. Therefore, keep it in your voice and completely centered on the first person singular. Write it as though you and I are sitting comfortably discussing the complexities of Engaged Leadership as they relate to the political, economic and social-cultural issues of society.
- It has been argued that one's ideas, thoughts, beliefs and opinions can best be shared via narratives. You may find it useful to illustrate your points through stories. Your stories are the context and meaning of your thoughts on Engaged Leadership.

Underlying a Platform on Engaged Leadership

Parker Palmer informs our work: "When we choose to engage, not evade, the tension of our differences, we will become better equipped to participate in a government of, by, and for the people as we expand some of our key civic capacities:

- To listen to each other openly and without fear, learning how much we have in common despite our differences
- To deepen our empathy for the alien "other" as we enter imaginatively into the experiences of people whose lives are radically unlike our own
- To hold what we believe and know with conviction and be willing to listen openly to other viewpoints, changing our minds if needed
- To seek our alternative facts and explanations whenever we find reason to doubt our own truth claims or the claims made by others, thus becoming better informed
- To probe, question, explore, and engage in dialogue, developing a fuller, more three-dimensional view of reality in the process
- To enter the conflicted arena of politics, able to hold the dynamics of that complex force field in ways that unite the civic community and empower us to hold governmental accountable to the will of the people
- To welcome opportunities to participate in collective problem solving and decision making, generating better solutions and making better decisions as we work with competing ideas
- To feel more at home on the face of the earth amid differences and many sorts, better able to enjoy the fruits of diversity.

The Platform

It is tempting to view notions of engaged leadership from a purely scientific or maybe even from some set of clearly understood rules. In reality, however, notions of engaged leadership are very complex. A platform implies something that supports one's beliefs and by which one justifies or validates one's own actions. A platform on Engaged Leadership helps an individual bring to the fore his/her thoughts on this complex issue and often brings clarity to much needed change. Your platform should address the following questions.

1. What are the major attributes that determine one's identity and why?
2. What are the political, economic, and social-cultural factors that impact one's thinking about differences among individuals?
3. Given the answers to the first two questions, how have your thoughts about diversity, inclusion and engaged leadership changed and how will your answers cause you to become a stronger advocate for a better society and world, for all?

REFERENCES:

Carnes, K., Cottrell, D. and Layton, M. (2004). Management Insights: Discovering the Truths to Management Success. Dallas, Texas: Corner Stone Publishing.

Palmer, P. (2011). Healing the Heart of Democracy. San Francisco, CA. Jossey-Bass.

Peet, M. Reynolds-Keefer, L. Gurin, P. and Lonn, S. Fall 2011/Winter (2012). Fostering Integrative Knowledge and Lifelong Learning. In: peerReview – Vol. 13, NO. 4/ Vol. 14, NO. 1. Washington, DC: Association of American Colleges and Universities.

CPSIA information can be obtained at www.ICGtesting.com
Printed in the USA
BVOW010859150213

313381BV00002B/5/P